The North American Fourth Edition

Cambridge Latin Course

Units 3 and 4

fābulae ancillantēs

Stan Farrow
Formerly of the David and Mary Thomson Collegiate Institute, Scarborough, Ontario, Canada

GENERAL EDITOR

Patricia E. Bell
Formerly of Centennial Collegiate and Vocational Institute, Guelph, Ontario, Canada

CAMBRIDGE
UNIVERSITY PRESS

CAMBRIDGE UNIVERSITY PRESS
Cambridge, New York, Melbourne, Madrid, Cape Town, Singapore, São Paulo

Cambridge University Press
32 Avenue of the Americas, New York NY 10013-2473, USA

www.cambridge.org
Information on this title: www.cambridge.org/9780521705158

© University of Cambridge School Classics Project 2007

First published 2007

Printed in the United States of America

ISBN 978-0-521-70515-8 paperback

Preface

Stories that serve! This collection of ancillary Latin passages is designed to supplement the *Cambridge Latin Course*. The stories can be used to provide extra practice in translation and/or comprehension or to provide material for evaluation purposes on tests or examinations. They served both purposes in the classes for which I composed them during the 20-plus years I enjoyed teaching the *CLC*.

Since the aim of any reading course, like the *CLC*, is to learn a language by reading it, the test of its success must come by evaluating how well students can indeed read and understand connected passages of that language. The fact that the textbook passages are so interesting in the *CLC* is a major factor in its success. But what does the teacher do when the need arises for extra practice or evaluation? Where does one turn to find more stories in the Cambridge style, with vocabulary and language features presented in the same order as the textbook series?

My solution was to make up my own, usually featuring further escapades by the *CLC* cast of characters. Soon I was sharing these with other teachers in my city and then beyond. Eventually the North American Cambridge Classics Project Resource Center published a selection of them under the skilled editorship of Pat Bell. It is that collection, revised to match the changes in the North American Fourth Edition of the *CLC*, that forms the basis for this booklet. Once again, my colleague and Canadian compatriot, Pat Bell, is at the editorial helm.

Most of these stories began life on tests or examinations and then became a resource for review or extra practice in later years. In Units 3 and 4, the vast majority are longer two-part stories, since the new language features in these Units, unlike the concentration on cases of nouns and tenses of verbs in Units 1 and 2, involve longer sentence structures like the uses of the subjunctive and various forms of indirect speech. Also, to match the unfolding story line in the Student's Texts, there is a balanced mixture of the serious and the not-so-serious. The Answer Key will sometimes explain the local events which inspired a particular narrative.

One word of caution, however. Unlike the stories in the *CLC*, this collection is not a continuous narrative, arising as it has from unconnected evaluation sessions with different classes in different years. Some of the stories may actually contradict others or at least seem inconsistent. No one group of my students ever read all of these stories and I would suggest you follow suit. The Answer Key also includes a few warnings about overlap or contradiction.

Teachers may note that a few Stages are not represented by stories. It was my custom in Unit 3 to give tests every two Stages and in Unit 4 to vary the procedure depending on the curriculum and time restraints of a particular year. The school calendar and the timing of term-end examinations would also be a factor. With usually slight changes to language and vocabulary content, many stories can be adapted to suit a near-by Stage, if necessary.

In glossing vocabulary for the stories, I have followed the usual *CLC* custom of including every word which has not appeared on a Checklist. Teachers are free to omit words from the glosses if it is felt that they are unnecessary. In two-part stories, vocabulary which is glossed in Part I is not glossed in Part II if it appears again there. The comprehension section of the stories (usually Part II) often allowed for inclusion of some sentences and phrases (including poetry) which might prove difficult to translate, but somewhat easier to comprehend. Judge accordingly.

Teachers may want to do some cutting and pasting to prepare a master copy of the version they wish to use with their students as stories do not always fit neatly onto one page.

A number of these stories, in whole or in part, appear in *Stage Tests 3* and *Stage Tests 4*. While the wording is not identical, because of differences in adapting the stories for the Fourth Edition, it would be unwise to use a story from one before a "test" from the other, where students are expected to be seeing the Latin for the first time. However, using the TestCrafter software from Cambridge University Press, teachers could mix and match stories and follow-up questions, to avoid overlap.

The following stories appear in *Stage Tests 3* and *Stage Tests 4*: 22.2 (used in the Stage 23 test); 22.3 II (except for the first two paragraphs); 24.1 I; 25.1 I; 26.3 I; 27.2 I and II; 30.4 I and II; 31.1 I and first half of II; 32.3 I; 32.4 I and first half of II (used in the Stage 33 test); 34.2 I and II; 36.1 I and II; 38.2 I and II; 39.1 I and II, with a large omission in the middle of II, summarized in an English paragraph; 40.1 I and II.

In addition to thanking Pat Bell for her editorial encouragement, I wish to acknowledge that this project would not have seen the light of day without a patient but persistent push from Fiona Kelly at Cambridge University Press. I also owe a debt of thanks to Richard Popeck, another member of our Fourth Edition revision team, who conveniently had much of the old NACCP material from this collection on disk and saved me hours by sharing it with me. Finally, of course, my appreciation to the many students whose interests, idiosyncracies, and initiatives inspired most of these stories. Please feel free to change, adapt, and otherwise modify any of them to help your own students share that same enthusiasm. And if, by chance, you too feel inspired to create your own collection, *euge*!

Stan Farrow

4

Modestus dēfīxiōnem invenit

Translate the following story.

Modestus, postquam sē ē fonte extrāxit, ibi stābat, Vilbiam Bulbumque
vituperāns. subitō aliquem thermās intrantem audīvit. mīles perterritus
post columnam sē cēlāvit, unde senātōrem Rōmānum cōnspexit.

    senātor, thermās ingressus, fontī tacitē appropinquāvit, dēfīxiōnem
portāns. tum, postquam dēfīxiōnem in fontem iactāvit, celeriter exiit.   5

    Modestus, quod iam madidus erat, in fontem dēsiluit et dēfīxiōnem ā
senātōre dēiectam invēnit. haec verba lēgit: necesse est Cogidubnō perīre.

dēfīxiōnem: dēfīxiō *curse tablet*	**columnam: columna** *column*
aliquem: aliquis *someone*	**madidus** *soaked through*
thermās: thermae *the baths*	

Modestus mendāx

Translate the following story.

Strȳthiō per viās oppidī Aquārum Sūlis ambulābat, amīcum Modestum
petēns. subitō mīlitem ē thermīs exeuntem cōnspexit. Modestus madidus
lentē prōcēdēbat.

    "Modeste!" clāmāvit Strȳthiō. "cūr tam madidus es? quis hoc fēcit?"

    Modestus Strȳthiōnī dēfīxiōnem ostendit, quam in fonte invēnerat.   5

    "iste Bulbus," inquit, "mē dēcēpit. hodiē ad thermās vēnit, hanc
dēfīxiōnem portāns. thermās ingressus, dēfīxiōnem in fontem dēiēcit.
verba in dēfīxiōne scrīpta deae Sūlī placuērunt. dea mē in fontem trāxit."

thermīs: thermae *the baths*	**dēfīxiōnem: dēfīxiō** *curse tablet*
madidus *soaked through*	

mīlitēs fortissimī

I

Translate the following story.

Modestus, mīles miserrimus, in tabernā Terentiī sedēbat. (tabernam
Latrōnis vīsitāre nunc timēbat!) pōculum vīnī hauriēns, hoc sibi cōgitāvit:
    "ā Bulbō dēceptus, in fontem sacrum dēcidī. paene periī, quod haec
aqua calidissima erat. Vilbia, thermās ingressa, clāmōrēs meōs audīvit et
mē valdē vituperāvit. nunc omnēs amīcī mē dērīdent."   5
    subitō Strȳthiō tabernam intrāvit, Modestum quaerēns. Modestus,
quod Strȳthiōnem prius cōnspexit, clāmāvit:
    "Strȳthiō, hūc venī! volō tē mē adiuvāre. nōlī recūsāre! es vir magnae
calliditātis. quō modō istum Bulbum pūnīre possum?"
    "ō Modeste," respondit amīcus, "nimium vīnī bibistī. mīles ēbrius   10
nūllōs hostēs superāre potest. tamen mē audī! cōnsilium optimum, ā deā
Sūle missum, habeō."

Terentiī: Terentius *Terentius*	**calliditātis: calliditās** *cleverness, shrewdness*
calidissima: calidus *hot*	**nimium** *too much*
thermās: thermae *the baths*	**ēbrius** *drunk*
prius *first*	

II

Read the rest of the story and answer the questions at the end.

Modestus, ā Strȳthiōne monitus, pōculum in mēnsam posuit et tacēbat,
amīcum audiēns.
    "necesse est nōbīs," inquit Strȳthiō, "dēfīxiōnem facere. hanc
dēfīxiōnem, in tabulā scrīptam, in fontem sacrum dēicere possumus. tum,
deam precātī, ultiōnem exspectāre possumus. iste Bulbus tē ita pūnīvit; tū   5
eum ita pūnīre potes!"
    postrīdiē igitur duo amīcī ad thermās festīnāvērunt. tamen in iānuā
fontis cōnstitērunt. nam aliquis, prope fontem stāns, amulētum in aquam
dēiciēbat.
    "nōnne is est Salvius, senātor Rōmānus?" susurrāvit Modestus. "cūr   10
senātor ad hunc fontem venīre velit?"
    subitō Salvius, mīlitēs cōnspicātus, eōs fontī appropinquāre iussit.
vultūs eōrum intentē spectāns, rogāvit,
    "cūr ad fontem sacrum vēnistis? quid vultis? celeriter respondēte!"
    Modestus, mīles fortissimus, ad pavīmentum exanimātus dēcidit.   15
Strȳthiō tamen incēpit:
    "mī amīce, dēfīxiōnem in aquam dēicere volumus. nam Bulbus, vir
mendāx, amīcum meum dēcēpit et puellam eius surripuit. nunc..."

"caudex!" clāmāvit Salvius. "Britannī, hominēs barbarī, deae Sūlī crēdunt, sed Rōmānīs nōn decōrum est hās nūgās efficere." 20

tum ē thermīs celeriter contendit.

Strȳthiō, quī Salvium amulētum dēicientem vīderat, nihil dīxit. sed ad fontem prōgressus, hoc amulētum in aquā quaesīvit. amulētum tandem adeptus, attonitus lēgit: mortem rēgī Cogidubnō.

Strȳthiō prope Modestum dēcidit exanimātus! 25

dēfīxiōnem: dēfīxiō *curse (tablet)*
tabulā: tabula *tablet*
ultiōnem: ultiō *revenge*
aliquis *someone*
amulētum: amulētum *charm, amulet*
susurrāvit: susurrāre *whisper*

velit *would want*
vultūs: vultus *face, expression*
pavīmentum: pavīmentum *floor*
surripuit: surripere *steal*
caudex: caudex *blockhead, idiot*
nūgās: nūgae *nonsense*

Questions

1 What was Strythio's plan for getting revenge on Bulbus?
2 Why did he expect it to work?
3 Why did the two men stop before entering the sacred spring area?
4 What puzzled Modestus?
5 How did Modestus react when Salvius confronted him?
6 What opinions did Salvius express about the sacred spring?
7 Why would this have puzzled Strythio?
8 What did Strythio read on the charm?

I

Translate the following story.

Strȳthiō in tabernā Latrōnis in oppidō Aquīs Sūlis sedēbat. subitō
Modestus per iānuam ruit, clāmāns,
    "adiuvā mē, Strȳthiō! mihi necesse est mē celerrimē cēlāre!"
    "quid est, Modeste?" respondit amīcus. "numquam tē tam perterritum
vīdī."   5
    "nūntius, quem lēgātus mīsit, adest. mandāta portat, quae mē ad
castra revenīre iubent. Strȳthiō, es vir summae calliditātis. ad pugnam
revenīre nōlō. velim diūtius vīvere. ubi mē cēlāre possum?"
    Modestus, haec locūtus, paene lacrimāvit. Bulbus et Gutta, quī āleam
prope mēnsam Strȳthiōnis lūdēbant, vehementer rīsērunt. tamen Strȳthiō,   *10*
quod cōnsilium invenīre temptābat, nihil dīxit. tum, surgēns, Modestō,
    "venī mēcum," inquit, "ad templum Sūlis Minervae. hodiē dea tibi
favet. hodiē sacerdōs fīs."

lēgātus *commander*	**āleam lūdēbant: āleam lūdere** *play dice*
castra: castra *camp*	**invenīre** *devise*
calliditātis: calliditās *cleverness*	**fīs** *become*
velim *would like*	

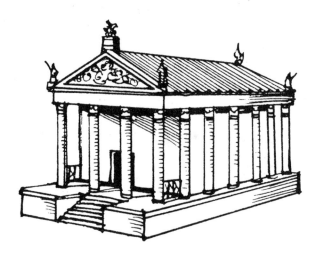

II

Read the rest of the story and answer the questions at the end.

Memor, prōcūrātor thermārum, in templō cum duōbus sacerdōtibus
victimam sacrificābat. Salvius, ubi in fānum irrūpit, Memorem iussit
sacerdōtēs dīmittere.

"sed, mī Salvī," inquit Memor, "necesse est nōbīs hunc gallum deae
Minervae sacrificāre. num velīs nōs deam offendere?"   5

"deam floccī nōn faciō!" respondit Salvius. "necesse est nōbīs sōlīs
dīcere. sacerdōtēs statim dīmitte!"

sacerdōtēs attonitī ā templō exiērunt. tum Salvius, postquam cautē
circumspectāvit, Memorī īrātus dīxit,

"stultissimē ēgistī, mī prōcūrātor. mortem omnibus nōbīs paene   10
prōcūrāvistī. cūr Cephalum dēlēgistī? tū ipse rem huius modī efficere
dēbuistī."

"sed Cephalus ipse hanc rem efficere voluit," respondit Memor.
"Cephalus ipse voluit mē sibi venēnum dare. Cephalus errāvit; ego nōn
errāvī. Cephalus erat vir minimae virtūtis."   15

"tū es vir minimae virtūtis," clāmāvit Salvius. "cūr tū 'Salvius...'
Cogidubnō dīcere incēpistī, postquam rēx tē ā cūrā thermārum dēmōvit?
velim cētera verba audīre. quid locūtūrus eras?"

"mī Salvī..."

"tacē!" susurrāvit Salvius. "aliquid post illam columnam videō."   20
Salvius ad columnam cucurrit. ibi Modestum trementem invēnit.

"quis est hic?" rogāvit. "quālis sacerdōs est?"

"nūllus sacerdōs est," respondit Memor. "est Modestus, mīles
aeger...et mīles ignāvissimus!"

"quid audīvistī?" Salvius postulāvit. "quid dīcēbāmus?"   25

"Cephalum...Cephalum..." sed Modestus plūs dīcere nōn potuit.

"quid dē Cephalō scīs?" Salvius rogāvit.

"Memor Cephalum necāvit," clāmāvit Modestus. "Memor eī venēnum
dedit. Memor Cogidubnō dīcere temptāvit, 'Salvius hoc fēcit...'"

"longē errās," coepit dīcere Memor, sed Salvius, "vērum dīcis," inquit.
"Memor hoc fēcit, sed Cephalus erat vir ingeniī prāvī. necesse erat   30
Memorī eum necāre. et tū nihil dē hāc rē dīcere dēbēs. nunc necesse est
mihi ad aulam Cogidubnī festīnāre, tibi Dēvam ad castra redīre. abī!"

Modestus ē templō quam celerrimē cucurrit. Salvius exiit rīdēns.
Memor in templō miserrimus stābat.

prōcūrātor *manager*	**locūtūrus** *going to say*
thermārum: thermae *baths*	**susurrāvit: susurrāre** *whisper*
fānum: fānum *shrine*	**trementem: tremere** *tremble*
gallum: gallus *rooster*	**quālis** *what kind of?*
prōcūrāvistī: prōcūrāre *procure*	**Dēvam** *to Deva, to Chester*
dēlēgistī: dēligere *choose*	

Questions

1 What was Memor doing at the beginning of this episode?
2 What order did Salvius issue?
3 What objection did Memor raise?
4 What trait of Salvius is revealed in his reply to Memor's objection?
5 What subject did Salvius wish to talk about?
6 How did he feel Memor should have handled the situation?
7 Whom did Memor blame for the failure of his plan, and why?
8 What action on Memor's part was Salvius especially curious about?
9 What surprising development cut short this conversation?
10 How did Memor describe the intruder?
11 What mistaken impression had the intruder gained?
12 How did Salvius "explain" the "truth"?
13 Explain why **Salvius exiit rīdēns.**

24.1   mīles perterritus

I

Translate the following story.

Modestus, cum sē ē fonte lentē extrāxisset, Strȳthiōnem quaerere voluit.

"necesse est nōbīs Dēvam redīre," inquit, "quod in hōc oppidō omnēs puellae mē dērīdēre nunc possunt. ā Bulbō dēceptus, homō trīstissimus sum!"

cum haec verba sibi dīceret, vōcēs īnfestōs subitō audīvit. mīles perterritus, deam timidē precātus, sē post columnam celerrimē cēlāvit, unde duōs virōs thermās intrantēs cōnspexit. Memorem senātōremque Rōmānum agnōvit, quī īrātī dissentiēbant. Modestus madidus miserrimusque humī iacēbat, hanc contentiōnem audiēns.

5

Dēvam *to Deva, to Chester*
columnam: columna *column*
thermās: thermae *the baths*
madidus *soaked through*
contentiōnem: contentiō *argument*

II

Read the rest of the story and answer the questions at the end.

"caudex!" clāmābat senātor. "cūr tū Cephalum dēlēgistī? tū ipse rem huius modī efficere dēbuistī."

"sed Cephalus ipse hanc rem efficere voluit," respondit Memor. "Cephalus ipse voluit mē sibi venēnum dare. Cephalus errāvit; ego nōn errāvī. Cephalus erat vir minimae virtūtis." 5

"tū es vir minimae virtūtis," clāmāvit Salvius. "cūr tū 'Salvius...' Cogidubnō dīcere incēpistī, cum rēx tē ā cūrā thermārum dēmōvisset? velim cētera verba audīre. quid locūtūrus erās?"

"mī Salvī..."

subitō Modestus sternuit. Memor Salviusque celeriter 10
circumspectāvērunt. ad columnam prōgressī, Modestum trementem invēnērunt.

"quis est hic?" rogāvit Salvius. "quālis sacerdōs est?"

"nūllus sacerdōs est," respondit Memor. "est Modestus, mīles aeger...et mīles ignāvissimus!" 15

"quid audīvistī?" Salvius postulāvit. "quid dīcēbāmus?"

"Cephalum...Cephalum..." sed Modestus plūs dīcere nōn potuit.

"quid dē Cephalō scīs?" Salvius rogāvit.

"Memor Cephalum necāvit," clāmāvit Modestus. "Memor eī venēnum dedit. Memor Cogidubnō dīcere temptāvit, 'Salvius hoc fēcit...'" 20

"longē errās," coepit dīcere Memor, sed Salvius, "vērum dīcis," inquit. "Memor hoc fēcit, sed Cephalus erat vir ingeniī prāvī. necesse erat Memorī eum necāre. et tū nihil dē hāc rē dīcere dēbēs. tūne intellegis?"

"bene intellegō," respondit Modestus, quī nihil intellēxit, nihil intellegere voluit. 25

"nunc," inquit Salvius, "necesse est mihi ad aulam Cogidubnī festīnāre, tibi Dēvam redīre. abī!"

Modestus ē thermīs quam celerrimē cucurrit. Salvius exiit rīdēns. Memor ibi miserrimus stābat.

caudex: caudex *blockhead, idiot*	**sternuit: sternuere** *sneeze*
dēlēgistī: dēligere *choose*	**prōgressī: prōgressus** *having proceeded,*
dēmōvisset: dēmovēre *remove,*	*having advanced*
dismiss	**trementem: tremere** *tremble*
velim *would like*	**quālis** *what kind of?*
locūtūrus *going to say*	

Questions

1 What apparently was the subject of the argument between Memor and the senator?
2 How did Salvius feel Memor should have handled the situation being discussed?
3 How did Memor explain having handled it the way he did?
4 What action on Memor's part was Salvius especially curious about?
5 Outline the mistaken version of the story Modestus had pieced together from overhearing the argument.
6 What explanation did Salvius offer, to convince Modestus that his version was correct?
7 Explain why, at the end of this episode, **Salvius exiit rīdēns**.

25.1 Strȳthiō auxilium offert

I

Translate the following story.

Modestus et Strȳthiō, ē carcere ēgressī, ad horrea festīnāre coepērunt. nam Strȳthiō, vir summae prūdentiae, explicāverat quō modō sub horreō sē cēlāre possent. tamen, duo mīlitēs, cum per castra tacitē prōcēderent, subitō hominem per portam intrantem cōnspexērunt. Modestus, quod intellēxit quis esset homō, Strȳthiōnī susurrāvit:

"necesse est nōbīs hinc effugere! hic enim est Salvius, vir magnae   5
auctōritātis. cum in istum fontem in oppidō Aquīs Sūlis cecidissem, dēfīxiōnem ā Salviō parātam invēnī. ille rēgem Cogidubnum necāre vult."

susurrāvit: susurrāre *whisper*   **cecidissem: cadere** *fall*
hinc *from here*

12

II

Read the rest of the story and answer the questions at the end.

Modestus, cum haec verba dīxisset, post aedificium proximum sē cēlāvit,
quod Salvium vītāre voluit. Strȳthiō tamen, mīles summae virtūtis, Salviō
audācter appropinquāvit.

"salvē, mī senātor!" inquit. "quid quaeris?"

"salvē, amīce!" respondit Salvius. "ego ad castra modo pervēnī.   5
necesse est mihi ad prīncipia festīnāre, quod Agricola mē exspectat.
necesse est tibi mē ad prīncipia dūcere."

Strȳthiō, cum haec audīvisset, valdē timēbat.

"ad prīncipia cum hōc senātōre īre nōlō," sēcum cōgitāvit, "quod iste
centuriō, Valerius, mē ibi cōnspicātus, comprehendere potest."   10

mīles, quod nesciēbat quid dīcere posset, immōtus stābat. Salvius
īrātius clāmābat:

"cūr ibi stās, caudex? nōnne prīncipia invenīre potes? senātor
potentissimus sum, quī dē rēbus gravissimīs cum Agricolā dīcere velim."

subitō Strȳthiō cōnsilium callidum cēpit.   15

"hīc maneō, domine," inquit, "quod amīcum meum exspectō. nōs tē
ad prīncipia statim dūcere possumus. amīcus meus aedificia reficere solet.
nunc post illud aedificium labōrat. heus! comes!"

Modestus īrātissimus perterritusque ad Strȳthiōnem Salviumque lentē
ambulāvit, amīcum tacitē vituperāns. Salvius interim, mīlitem intentē   20
spectāns,

"nōnne tē agnōscō?" rogāvit. "in oppidō Aquīs Sūlis..."

"erat frāter meus...Herculēs!" celeriter respondit Modestus. "frāter
saepe thermās vīsitat, quod vir aegerrimus est."

tum, ad Strȳthiōnem versus,   25

"pestis!" susurrāvit, "cūr mē arcessīvistī? quid facis?"

Strȳthiō tamen Salvium ad horrea dūcere coepit.

"ecce! prīncipia!" inquit.

Salvius, iam īrātissimus, clāmāvit:

"caecusne es? haec aedificia sunt horrea, nōn prīncipia!"   30

"ita vērō," respondit Strȳthiō. "haec aedificia simillima horreīs sunt.
tamen rē vērā prīncipia sunt. Britannī saepe haec castra oppugnant.
prīncipia incendere volunt. itaque prīncipia horreīs simillima fēcimus et
Britannōs ita dēcēpimus."

tum Strȳthiō centuriōnem Valerium ē prīncipiīs vērīs exeuntem   35
cōnspexit. mīles Modestum sēcum dūxit et post aedificia contendit,
Salvium mediā in viā relinquēns. Salvius attonitus sibi cōgitāvit,

"sī tālēs mīlitēs imperium Rōmānum custōdiunt, summō in perīculō
sumus!"

proximum: proximus *near-by*
modo *just now*
prīncipia: prīncipia *headquarters*
caudex: caudex *blockhead, idiot*
velim *would like*
hīc *here*
reficere *repair*
heus! *hey!*

comes: comes *comrade*
thermās: thermae *the baths*
susurrāvit: susurrāre *whisper*
caecus *blind*
simillima: similis *like, similar*
rē vērā *in fact*
vērīs: vērus *true, real*
tālēs: tālis *such, like this/these*

Questions

1 Contrast the behavior of Modestus and Strythio in the first paragraph.
2 What did Salvius want Strythio to do?
3 Why did Strythio not want to do this?
4 What ingenious explanation did Strythio provide for Modestus' being behind the building?
5 What explanation did Modestus provide when Salvius thought he recognized him?
6 Where did Strythio take Salvius?
7 When Salvius complained, what ingenious explanation did Strythio provide?
8 Why did Strythio and Modestus run off?

26.1 Agricola et Imperātor

I

Translate the following story.

Agricola in prīncipiīs sōlus sedēbat, verba Salviī cōgitāns. valdē
commōtus erat, quod nesciēbat num hic senātor Rōmānus vēra dīceret.
  "istī Salviō nōn crēdō," sibi dīxit. "nam vir minimae fideī est.
Imperātor Domitiānus tamen eum ad Britanniam mīsit ut rēgnum
Cogidubnī īnspiceret...et occupāret? mihi cavendum est, quod Imperātor   5
novus, quī virō huius modī crēdit, aut īnsānus aut scelestus est."

cavendum: cavēre *beware*

aut...aut... *either...or...*

14

II

Read the rest of the story and answer the questions at the end.

Agricola, haec verba sibi locūtus, epistulam scrībere cōnstituit ut ad
Imperātōrem mitteret:

"Gnaeus Iūlius Agricola, lēgātus Augustī prōpraetor Imperātōrī
Domitiānō Augustō, Dīvī Vespasiānī fīliō salūtem dīcit.

"gaudeō, domine, quod tibi victōriās optimās, nōmine tuō dignās   5
referō. pater tuus, Vespasiānus, mē ad hanc īnsulam mīsit ut pācem
Britannīs impōnerem. cum Britanniam quīnque annōs administrāvissem,
tōtam īnsulam occupāre poteram, praeter Calēdoniam. bellum igitur
contrā Calēdoniōs mihi gerendum erat. nāvēs ēmīsī ut portūs barbarōrum
explōrārem; ego ipse simul in Calēdoniam multīs cum mīlitibus prōcessī.   10

"Calēdoniī fortissimī omnium Britannōrum sunt. tamen, quamquam
fortiter resistēbant et, castra nostra noctū ingressī, multōs Rōmānōs
necāvērunt, eōs tandem superāre poterāmus. paucī fūgērunt; quī domōs
suās incendērunt, uxōrēs līberōsque interfēcērunt, quod nōlēbant eōs esse
servōs. postrīdiē nūllōs barbarōs invenīre poterāmus nisi mortuōs.   15

"hanc victōriam tibi nūntiāre cōnstituī ut nōbīscum gaudērēs. mīlitēs
tuī, mīlitēs Rōmānī, tōtam Britanniam nunc occupant!"

cōnstituit: cōnstituere *decide*
lēgātus Augustī prōpraetor *governor*
  of the imperial province
salūtem dīcit *sends greetings*
gaudeō: gaudēre *rejoice, be happy*
victōriās: victōria *victory*
dignās: dignus *worthy*
impōnerem: impōnere *impose*
praeter *except*

Calēdoniam: Calēdonia *Caledonia*
  (modern Scotland)
contrā *against*
explōrārem: explōrāre *explore, scout*
simul *at the same time*
noctū *at night*
līberōs: līberī *children*
nisi *except, unless*

Questions

1 The salutation of Agricola's letter is long and formal. That length allows Agricola to work in some titles or phrases designed to influence Domitian's reaction. Select one such item and explain the effect Agricola would want it to have.

2 In his first paragraph Agricola reports on **victōriās optimās nōmine tuō dignās**. How is this designed to influence the emperor?

3 What did Agricola feel his mandate was in Britain?

4 How would that justify his action in Caledonia?

5 What was one advance preparation he made for the campaign against the Caledonians?

6 What was one set-back during the campaign which he reported?

7 What two actions did the Caledonian fugitives take?

8 Why did they do this?

26.2   Vincēns

I

Translate the following story.

Agricola cum Sīlānō, lēgātō legiōnis, et cum tribūnīs colloquium habēbat. hī virī enim, mīlitēs summae auctōritātis, in prīncipiīs convēnerant ut dē Vincente, mīlite novō, dīcerent. Sīlānus, epistulam tenēns, Agricolae explicāvit cūr eum ad hoc concilium arcessīvisset:

5

"Vincēns, cum ad haec castra pervēnisset, nōs maximē dēlectāre solēbat. nam, ad bellum missus, semper fortiter pugnābat. herī tamen Rūfus, tribūnus fidēlissimus, prīncipia ingressus, mihi hanc epistulam ostendit, ab amīcō scrīptam. spectā haec verba: 'Vincēns est servus. nōlī servum in exercitū retinēre!' quid factūrī sumus? nōbīs cōnstituendum est."

10

15

concilium: concilium *meeting*
exercitū: exercitus *army*

factūrī: factūrus *going to do*
cōnstituendum: cōnstituere *decide*

II

Read the rest of the story and answer the questions at the end.

Agricola, cum epistulam intentē lēgisset, rem sēcum cōgitābat. deinde
sententiam nūntiāvit:

"Vincentī, sī haec verba vēra sunt, ad Ītaliam redeundum est. nōn
decōrum est servīs in exercitū pugnāre. iuvenem ad prīncipia statim
vocā!"   5

Rūfus tribūnus exiit ut mīlitem invenīret. Vincēns, ad prīncipia
arcessītus, alacriter hīs mandātīs pāruit. in animō volvit num lēgātus
cōnstituisset praemium sibi dare, quod tam fortiter pugnāvisset. tamen
vultūs gravēs lēgātī tribūnōrumque cōnspicātus, anxius celeriter fīēbat.

Agricola, Vincentī epistulam ostendēns, rogāvit,   10

"haec verba vidēs? haec verba sunt vēra?"

"linguam Latīnam nōn bene intellegō," respondit iuvenis. "mihi verba
lege!"

"sī linguam Latīnam nōn bene intellegis," inquit Agricola, "haec verba
quidem vēra sunt. tū es servus."   15

"quis tibi hoc dīxit?" clāmāvit Vincēns. "cēterīne mīlitēs mē
prōdidērunt? multī mīlitum mihi invident, quod mīles summae virtūtis
summīque studiī sum! inīquum est!"

tum iuvenis lacrimāre coepit.

Agricola, lacrimās neglegēns, Vincentem haec iussit: 20

"tibi ad contubernium redeundum, ē castrīs discēdere parandum est.
necesse est mihi eōs pūnīre quī mandāta Imperātōris neglegunt; necesse
est tibi mandātīs meīs pārēre."

vēra: vērus *true, real*
alacriter *eagerly*
in animō volvit: in animō volvere
  wonder
praemium: praemium *reward*
vultūs: vultus *face*
anxius *anxious, worried*
fīēbat *became*

quidem *indeed*
prōdidērunt: prōdere *betray*
invident: invidēre *be jealous of*
studiī: studium *enthusiasm*
inīquum: inīquus *unfair*
neglegēns: neglegere *ignore*
contubernium: contubernium
  barracks

Questions

1 What judgment was Agricola prepared to hand down if the accusation in the letter proved true?
2 What reason did he give for this decision?
3 Why was Vincent so eager to meet with his commanding officer?
4 What was the first sign that his eagerness might be misplaced?
5 How did he first avoid admitting the truth?
6 Judging by the way Agricola interpreted Vincent's comment, why was that technique (the answer to 5) a mistake?
7 Whom did Vincent blame for his predicament, and why?
8 What order did Agricola give Vincent?
9 According to Agricola's last statement, how did he see his role as governor of a Roman province?

26.3 Quīntus exīre parat

I

Translate the following story.

Quīntus, cum dē morte Cogidubnī audīvisset, ad prīncipia contendit ut Rūfum quaereret. ibi tribūnus mīlitum colloquium cum Agricolā dē rēge mortuō habēbat. prīncipia ingressus, Quīntus lēgātum tribūnumque salūtāvit.

"salvēte, amīcī! vōsne quoque trīstissimī estis quod vir maximae fideī   5
periit? nōs Rōmānōs oportet numquam huius amīcī bonī immemorēs esse.

"nunc autem mihi ad Ītaliam redeundum est. pater tuus, Rūfe, mē ad hanc īnsulam mīsit ut tē invenīrem. hoc iam fēcī. Dumnorix mē ad haec castra mīsit ut Cogidubnum adiuvārem. hoc nōn iam facere possum. perīculōsum est mihi in Britanniā manēre, quod Salvius, vir ingeniī prāvī,   10
mē pūnīre vult."

Agricola et Rūfus, cum cognōvissent quid Quīntus facere vellet, eī auxilium prōmīsērunt.

nōn iam *no longer*   **perīculōsum: perīculōsus** *dangerous*

18

II

Read the rest of the story and answer the questions at the end.

Quīntus iter ad urbem Rōmam facere statuerat ut colloquium cum
Imperātōre habēret. cōnsilium Rūfō explicāvit:
  "istī Salviō nōn crēdō. num Domitiānus rēgnum Cogidubnī occupāre
voluit? nōnne Imperātōrī tōtam rem nārrāre possum? necesse est Salviō
poenās dare. Imperātor sōlus rem huius modī administrāre potest. itaque   5
mihi ad Urbem festīnandum est."
  "quamquam Salviō nōn crēdis," respondit Rūfus, "tē oportet
Domitiānum quoque cavēre. nam Cogidubnus erat amīcus Claudiī,
amīcus Vespasiānī, nōn Domitiānī amīcus. Imperātor novus virīs
iuveniōribus favet; fortasse ūnus hōrum iuvenum est Salvius. sī Salvius   10
vērum dīcit, tibi cavendum est."
  cum Rūfus haec verba dīceret, Agricola, ad prīncipia regressus,
nūntiāvit,
  "ego Valeriō, centuriōnī optimō, mandāta dedī. ille equum parāvit; ita
tū ad lītus celeriter equitāre potes. custōdēs quoque quaesīvit; illī tē per   15
viās perīculōsās dūcere possunt. duōs mīlitēs fortēs habēbat quī carcerem
custōdiēbant; hōs mīlitēs autem quaesītōs invenīre nōn potest. tibi hīc
manendum est dum Valerius eōs inveniat; tum ad Ītaliam tūtus prōcēdere
potes."

statuerat: statuere *decide*   hīc *here*
cavēre *beware*   dum inveniat *until he can find*
lītus: lītus *shore*

19

Questions

1 Quintus explained his plan to Rufus:
    a Of what situation in Britain was he skeptical?
    b What did he hope to be able to do in Rome?
    c Why did he feel this was a necessary step?
2 Rufus was not as skeptical as Quintus:
    a What did he say about the changed political situation in Rome?
    b What warning did he give Quintus?
3 Agricola had already been making arrangements for Quintus' journey:
    a What was one preparation which had been completed?
    b What was one preparation which was still being worked on?
    c Who might the **duōs mīlitēs fortēs ... quī carcerem custōdiēbant** have been?
    d How would that make Agricola's last comment at the end of the passage ironic?

26.4   Rūfus attonitus

I

Translate the following story. It outlines what might have happened when Rufus was sent to interview Quintus.

Rūfus, ē prīncipiīs ēgressus, ad valētūdinārium contendit. nam medicus quem Agricola arcessīverat Quīntum eō mīserat ut vulnus eius cūrāret. tribūnus, cum valētūdinārium intrāvisset, iuvenem in lectō prope fenestram iacentem cōnspexit. ad lectum prōgressus, rogāre parābat cūr Quīntus ad castra vulnerātus squālidusque vēnisset. Quīntus tamen in animō volvēbat num hic mīles sibi crēditūrus esset. paulīsper ambō, inter sē īnspicientēs, nihil dīxērunt.   5

valētūdinārium: valētūdinārium
  hospital
eō *there (to that place)*
fenestram: fenestra *window*
prōgressus *having advanced*

squālidus *filthy*
in animō volvēbat: in animō volvere
  wonder
crēditūrus *going to believe*
ambō *both*

II

Read the rest of the story and answer the questions which follow.

Rūfus prīmus, "salvē!" inquit. "ego sum Rūfus, tribūnus Rōmānus.
Agricola mē ad tē mīsit ut quam plūrima dē tē cognōscerem. Agricola
enim..."

    subitō Quīntus exclāmāvit, "Rūfus? dīc mihi, ubi habitābās antequam
mīlitāre coepistī?"   5

    Rūfus haesitāns, "Alexandrīae," respondit. "cūr rogās?"

    "patrisne tuī nōmen erat Barbillus?"

    "ita vērō! quō modō hoc scīs? quid dē patre meō audīvistī?"

    iam Rūfus permōtus Quīntum interrogāre coepit. ille tamen, digitum
ad labrum tollēns, epistulam in mēnsā iacentem dēmōnstrāvit. Rūfus   10
epistulam adeptus, avidē perlēgit. prīmō tam mōtus erat ut nihil dīcere
posset. deinde, paene lacrimāns,

    "amīce," inquit, "tibi maximās grātiās agō quod tot beneficia patrī
meō praestitistī. tū quidem vir summae virtūtis es. nunc mihi ad prīncipia
redeundum est et Agricolae dīcendum est omnia quae dē Quīntō Caeciliō   15
Iūcundō sciō!"

    Rūfus, haec locūtus, ē valētūdināriō quam celerrimē exiit ut Agricolam
certiōrem faceret.

antequam *before*
mīlitāre *serve in the army*
permōtus *very excited*
digitum: digitus *finger*
labrum: labrum *lip*
perlēgit: perlegere *read through*

prīmō *at first*
beneficia: beneficium *kindness*
praestitistī: praestāre *show*
quidem *indeed*
certiōrem faceret: certiōrem facere
    inform

Questions

1 What did Rufus tell Quintus was the purpose of his visit?
2 Why did Quintus interrupt Rufus?
3 What two questions did he ask Rufus?
4 How did Rufus react after the second one?
5 Suggest one reason why Quintus pointed to the letter instead of telling the story himself.
6 What was Rufus' first reaction after reading the letter?
7 What did he then tell Quintus he (Rufus) had to do?

27.1 Salvius et custōdēs

I

Translate the following story.

Agricola, postquam dē morte Cogidubnī audīvit, Salvium statim dīmīsit.
ille, ē prīncipiīs ēgressus, sēcum cōgitābat,
  "mihi festīnandum est ad aulam Cogidubnī. dē testāmentō Cogidubnī
cognōscere volō."
  necesse erat Salviō equōs et custōdēs habēre ut ad aulam rēgis iter   5
faceret. tamen Agricolae patefacere nōluit quō contenderet. itaque hoc
cōnsilium cēpit:
  in cubiculō suō trēs hōrās manēbat. deinde,
cum advesperāsceret, ad centuriōnem Valerium
clam ībat. Valerius, quī nesciēbat dē morte   10
Cogidubnī, Salviō crēdidit. tam cupidus
adiuvandī erat ut eī duōs custōdēs optimōs daret:
Modestum et Strȳthiōnem!

testāmentō: testāmentum *will*
advesperāsceret: advesperāscere *get dark*
clam *secretly*
cupidus adiuvandī *eager to help*

II

Read the rest of the story and answer the questions at the end.

Salvius cum duōbus custōdibus per tenebrās ad aulam Cogidubnī
equitābat. Modestus, quod Salvium agnōvit, perterritus erat. in animō
volvēbat num Salvius sē agnitūrus esset. nam Salvius eum in templō

Aquīs Sūlis vīderat. Salvius tamen, quod per tenebrās custōdēs vidēre nōn poterat, dē Cogidubnō sōlō cōgitāns, Modestum nōn agnōvit. 5

post paucās hōrās ad flūmen altum vēnērunt. Salvius custōdēs rogāvit ubi esset pōns.

"pōns quī hīc stābat erat sēmirutus," respondit Strȳthiō. "pondus grave eum dēlēvit." tum Modestum intentē spectāvit.

Salvius, quod ad aulam quam celerrimē advenīre voluit, custōdibus 10 imperāvit ut cognōscerent ubi flūmen trānsīre possent. duo mīlitēs, in silvās ēgressī, mox rettulērunt,

"facile est nōbīs hoc flūmen trānsīre. prope illās arborēs sunt multa saxa in aquā. hīs saxīs ūsī, ad alteram rīpam pervenīre possumus."

custōdēs Salvium ad saxa dūxērunt. ille Strȳthiōnem imperāvit ut 15 prīmus trānsīret. Strȳthiō tamen tam timidus erat ut recūsāret. Modestus quoque nōluit. Salvius igitur, ignāviam custōdum dētestātus, trānsīre coepit. subitō equus, in saxō lapsus, Salvium in aquam dēiēcit. ille mediīs ex undīs clāmāvit,

"caudicēs! mihi subvenīte!" 20

sed caudicēs nōn tam stultī erant ut ibi manērent. in silvās quam celerrimē fūgērunt.

Salvius, cum sē ex aquā madidus trāxisset, ad aulam prōcessit sōlus.

tenebrās: tenebrae *darkness*	**rettulērunt: referre** *bring back word, report back*
in animō volvēbat: in animō volvere *wonder*	**arborēs: arbor** *tree*
agnitūrus *going to recognize*	**ūsī: ūsus** *using, making use of*
altum: altus *deep*	**ignāviam: ignāvia** *cowardice*
hīc *here*	**dētestātus** *having cursed*
sēmirutus *half-collapsed*	**lapsus** *having slipped*
pondus *weight*	**subvenīte: subvenīre** *help*
	madidus *soaked through*

Questions

1 Why was Modestus terrified?
2 Why did he have good reason to be worried?
3 Why, as it turned out, were his worries unnecessary this time?
4 What problem did the three men encounter on their journey?
5 How did Strythio explain the situation?
6 What order did Salvius issue?
7 What report did Modestus and Strythio bring back?
8 What happened when Salvius tried to cross the river?
9 How did Modestus and Strythio react then?
10 How did this affect the rest of the trip for Salvius?

mīles miserrimus

I

Translate the following story.

Modestus, mīles miserrimus, in carcere sedēbat. nam lēgātus eī
imperāverat ut carcerem custōdīret. cum ibi sedēret, sibi cōgitābat:
   "cūr mihi hīc manendum est? haec vīta mihi odiō est. carcerem
custōdiēns, neque cibum cōnsūmere neque āleam lūdere neque puellās
pulchrās vīsitāre possum."   5
   cum haec verba sibi dīxisset, tam commōtus erat ut cōnsilium audāx
suscipere cōnstituit. amīcōs ad carcerem invītāre voluit ut āleam lūderent.
tamen, quod nesciēbat quō modō tantum cōnsilium suscipere posset,
necesse erat eī Strȳthiōnem cōnsulere.
   ille, ad carcerem arcessītus, quam celerrimē festīnāvit ut amīcum   10
adiuvāret.

hīc *here*   cōnstituit: cōnstituere *decide*
odiō est: odiō esse *be hateful*   cōnsulere *consult*
āleam lūdere *play dice*

II

Read the rest of the story and answer the questions at the end.

Strȳthiō, carcerem ingressus, cōnsilium Modestī audīvit. tamen, cum
cognōvisset quid amīcus in animō habēret, magnopere rīsit:
   "nihil facilius est! multae cellae dēsertae sunt, quō āleās, cibum...etiam
puellās ferre possumus. nōlī timēre! omnia cūrāre possum."
   haec verba locūtus, Strȳthiō ē carcere contendit ut mandāta Modestī   5
efficeret.
   postrīdiē, cum Modestus amīcōs exspectāret, centuriō Valerius
carcerem intrāvit ut cellās captīvōsque īnspiceret. quamquam Modestus
prope portam stāre voluit ut amīcōs monēret, centuriō rogāvit ut cellās
sibi dēmōnstrāret. cum ad cellam ultimam pervēnissent, subitō Strȳthiō,   10
amīcī, etiam puellae per portam contendērunt, cibum portantēs, multum
clāmantēs. tum Valerium cōnspicātī, cōnstitērunt perterritī.
   Valerius Modestum statim rogāvit cūr hī amīcī ad carcerem vēnissent:
   "num vōs āleam iterum lūditis? mīlitēs Rōmānōs non decet āleam in
carcere lūdere."   15
   "minimē, mī centuriō," respondit Modestus. "hī amīcī vēnērunt
ut...ut..."

24

"ut Modestō grātulātiōnēs darēmus," clāmāvit Strȳthiō, quī cōnsilium callidum cēperat. "Nigrīna, saltātrīx Britannica, Modestō nūbere vult. nōs Modestō grātulātiōnēs..." 20

"quid?" rogāvit Modestus, attonitus. (Modestus nūllam uxōrem habēre voluit!)

centuriō autem, quī rem bene intellēxerat, Modestō Nigrīnaeque (quae aderat) quoque grātulātus, Strȳthiōnī amīcīsque imperāvit ut cibum cōnsūmerent, āleam lūderent...et sacerdōtem arcesserent quī cōnūbium 25 sancīret. Modestus iterum mīles miserrimus erat!

in animō habēret: in animō
  habēre *have in mind*
cellae: cella *cell*
grātulātiōnēs: grātulātiōnēs
  congratulations
saltātrīx *dancer, dancing-girl*
nūbere *marry*
grātulātus *having congratulated*
cōnūbium sancīret: cōnūbium sancīre
  consecrate the marriage

Questions

1 What was Strythio's plan to implement Modestus' wishes?
2 What happened the next day to upset the scheme?
3 How did Modestus hope to prevent an embarrassing disaster?
4 What prevented him from being able to do this?
5 Describe the embarrassing event which therefore took place.
6 What did the centurion immediately suspect?
7 What cover story did Strythio suddenly think of as an explanation?
8 Why would this story come as a surprise to Modestus?
9 What unkind instruction did the centurion give, to prove that he understood the real situation?

I

Translate the following story.

Modestus, carcerī praefectus, tam commōtus erat ut nescīret quid facere
dēbēret. in animō volvit cūr lēgātus hoc 'praemium' sibi dedisset. cum
haec sēcum cōgitāret, subitō cōnsilium callidum cēpit. ē carcere ēgressus,
ad prīncipia contendit Sīlānumque rogāvit ut Strȳthiōnem quoque ad
carcerem mitteret ut sē adiuvāret.   5
    "Strȳthiō," inquit Modestus, "mīles est summae fideī. necesse est tibi
eī idem praemium dare."
    "mī Modeste," respondit Sīlānus, "paucī mīlitum meōrum fortiōrēs
sunt quam tū. mihi placet precēs tuās audīre. tibi ad amīcum festīnandum
est. dā eī mandāta mea! carcerem bene cūrāte!"   10
    lēgātus, haec verba locūtus, discessit ut cēterōs mīlitēs īnspiceret,
Modestus ut comitem quaereret.

praefectus: praeficere   *put in charge of*   **idem: īdem**   *the same*
in animō volvit: in animō volvere   *wonder*   **precēs: precēs**   *prayers, wishes*

II

Read the rest of the story and answer the questions at the end.

Modestus et Strȳthiō, carcerem administrantēs, colloquia inter sē habēre
solēbant. quondam, cum dē captīvīs dīcerent, Modestus rogāvit cūr illī
tam miserī essent ut effugere semper temptārent.
    "captīvī laetī effugere nōlunt," Strȳthiōnī inquit. "quō modō hōs
captīvōs laetōs reddere possumus?"   5
    "captīvus cuius cella est pulchra sānē laetus esse dēbet," respondit
Strȳthiō. "necesse est captīvīs cellās pingere corōnīsque rosārum ōrnāre!"

26

cum autem amīcī captīvīs imperāvissent ut hoc facerent, illī rosās in
pavīmentum dēiēcērunt, pigmentum in ōra custōdum!

deinde Strȳthiō aliud cōnsilium prōposuit: 10

"captīvus cui parum dēlectātiōnis dedimus sānē miser est. Nigrīnam
ex oppidō ad carcerem invītāre dēbēmus. saltātrīx captīvōs semper
dēlectat."

itaque Nigrīna, ab amīcīs arcessīta, ad carcerem festīnāvit ut captīvīs
saltāret. tamen, priusquam illa saltāre coepit, Modestus paucōs iocōs   15
dīcere cōnstituit. tam stultī erant iocī, tam raucī clāmōrēs captīvōrum, ut
Modestō tacendum, Nigrīnae lacrimantī effugiendum esset.

tandem Strȳthiō cōnsilium optimum habuit:

"hae cellae obscūrae sunt. captīvus quī in tenebrīs tōtum diem manet
laetus esse nōn potest."   20

itaque comitēs mūrum carceris sternere coepērunt ut fenestrās māiōrēs
facerent. captīvī autem, hanc occāsiōnem adeptī, per exitūs novōs
laetissimī ērūpērunt. Modestus, hoc cōnspicātus,

"ēheu!" inquit. "captīvī nunc laetī sunt, nōs miserrimī. iterum nōbīs
effugiendum est!"   25

reddere *make, render*	**saltātrīx** *dancing-girl*
cella *cell*	**priusquam** *before*
pingere *paint*	**cōnstituit: cōnstituere** *decide*
corōnīs: corōna *garland*	**raucī: raucus** *raucous, harsh*
rosārum: rosa *rose*	**obscūrae: obscūrus** *dark*
pavīmentum: pavīmentum *floor*	**tenebrīs: tenebrae** *darkness*
pigmentum: pigmentum *paint*	**sternere** *knock down*
prōposuit: prōpōnere *propose*	**fenestrās: fenestra** *window*
parum *too little*	**occāsiōnem: occāsiō** *opportunity, chance*
dēlectātiōnis: dēlectātiō *amusement,*	**exitūs: exitus** *exit, opening*
pleasure	**ērūpērunt: ērumpere** *burst out*

Questions

1 This story outlines a number of plans suggested by Strythio. What
  was the apparent purpose of them all?
2 It was Modestus who actually suggested this purpose when he asked
  for Strythio's advice at the beginning of the passage. What positive
  result did he suggest if they succeeded in this purpose?
3 For each of Strythio's first two plans, indicate:
  a the problem for the prisoners with which it attempted to deal
  b the suggested method of dealing with that problem
  c the reason why the plan did not succeed.
4 a What was the third plan?
  b What problem did it attempt to solve?
  c What was the result?
5 Explain how the ending of the story is ironic.

28.1   dolor Rūfillae

I

Translate the following story.

Salvius, cum iter per Britanniam multōs diēs fēcisset, pecūniam opēsque
extorquēns, tandem ad aulam revēnit. tam fessus erat ut ad cubiculum
festīnāret, quod dormīre volēbat. eī tamen occurrit uxor Rūfilla, īrā
dolōreque commōta. quae, cubiculum cum marītō ingressa, eum rogāvit
cūr sē dēseruisset.   5
    Salvius, hīs verbīs attonitus, Rūfillae imperāvit ut tacēret:
    "tē nōn decet marītum sīc vituperāre. ad cubiculum tuum tibi
redeundum est."

dolor *pain, sadness*   **extorquēns: extorquēre** *extort*

II

Read through the rest of the story and answer the questions at the end.

Rūfilla autem ē cubiculō exīre nōlēbat.
    "tibi placet," inquit, "iter per prōvinciam facere; tibi nōn placet
uxōrem tēcum dūcere. mē in hāc aulā, ventīs gelidīs verberātā, vōcibus
mīrābilibus complētā, sōlam relinquis!
    "cum abessēs, dormīre nōn poteram, quod somnia dīra mē terrēbant.   5
umbra rēgis Cogidubnī per cubiculum ambulābat, manūs sanguinolentās
vibrāns. rēx rogābat cūr Salvius eum occīdisset. cum surrēxissem ut
manūs rēgis lavārem, umbra ēvānuit. ō Salvī!
cūr illās manūs sanguinolentās lavāre nōn
poteram?"
    tum Rūfilla, marītum precāta ut aulam   10
vēnderet et ad Ītaliam redīret, lacrimīs sē dedit.
Salvius, metū uxōris commōtus, nesciēbat quid
sē dīcere oportēret. subitō nūntius, cubiculum
ingressus, Salviō epistulam ab Imperātōre
scrīptam trādidit. Imperātor Salviō imperāverat   15
ut ad urbem Rōmam redīret.

gelidīs: gelidus *cold, freezing*
somnia: somnium *dream*
sanguinolentās: sanguinolentus
   blood-stained, bloody
vibrāns: vibrāre *shake*
ēvānuit: ēvānēscere *vanish*

28

Questions

1 What did Rufilla suggest Salvius should have done when he went on his journey?
2 What were two complaints she made about the palace?
3 Outline what she saw in the dream she told to Salvius.
4 What did she try to do when she got up?
5 Why didn't she succeed in doing this?
6 What did she beg Salvius to do?
7 How did Salvius react to her request?
8 How did the message from the emperor solve Salvius' problems?

28.2 Modestus āthlēta

I

Translate the following story.

Gāius Iūlius Sīlānus, lēgātus legiōnis secundae, per viās castrōrum
ambulābat ut omnia aedificia īnspiceret. cum ad carcerem pervēnisset,
clāmōrēs magnōs audīvit. tantus erat clāmor ut Sīlānus statim ad portam
carceris contenderet. nam cognōscere voluit quid accideret. carcerem
ingressus, captīvīs imperāvit ut tacērent. cum illī hoc fēcissent, lēgātus   5
prīmae cellae appropinquāvit ut captīvum rogāret cūr omnēs clāmārent.
ille, metū perculsus, manūs suās ad mūrum extendit et "discus...discus..."
susurrāvit. nihil aliud dīcere poterat.

Sīlānus, coniūrātiōnem suspicātus, cēterōs Britannōs idem rogāre
cōnstituit. cum hoc faceret, subitō   10
sonitum terribilem audīvit. aliquid
mūrum carceris percusserat. statim
captīvī iterum clāmāre coepērunt.

lēgātus, clāmōre incēnsus, in
āream cucurrit ut cognōsceret quid   15
mūrum percussisset. duōs mīlitēs,
Modestum Strȳthiōnemque, mediā in
āreā agnōvit.

cellae: cella *cell*
perculsus *struck, overcome*
extendit: extendere *extend, point*
susurrāvit: susurrāre *whisper*
idem: īdem *the same*
terribilem: terribilis *terrible, terrifying*
percusserat: percutere *strike*
āream: ārea *courtyard*

29

II

Read the rest of the story and answer the questions at the end.

Strȳthiō Modestō discum trādēbat. tum Modestus prōcessit ut discum
ēmitteret. subitō lēgātum cōnspicātus, discum in terram ōmīsit. tam
attonitus erat ut ibi stāret immōtus.

Sīlānus mīlitibus appropinquāvit et īrātus rogāvit quid facerent.

"vōs carcerī praefēcī," clāmāvit. "cūr captīvōs nōn custōditis? cūr   5
discum in āreā ēmittitis? cūr captīvōs terrētis?"

Strȳthiō respondit,

"Modestus, amīcus meus, est āthlēta nōtissimus. discum longē
ēmittere potest. hōc annō lūdī Olympicī in Graeciā fīunt. Modestus
exercēbat ut prīmam palmam acciperet. nōbīs ad Graeciam abeundum   10
est!"

"caudicēs!" clāmāvit lēgātus. "mīlitēs Rōmānī in lūdīs Olympicīs nōn
certant. eī quī in Britanniā mīlitant ad Graeciam nōn abeunt. vōs oportet
ad carcerem redīre."

subitō omnēs magnum clāmōrem ē carcere audīvērunt. Vercobrix,   15
fīlius prīncipis Britannicī, iterum fugere temptābat. custōdem aggressus,
iam per portam apertam currēbat. Sīlānus, hunc cōnspicātus, statim per
āream ruēbat. Modestus tamen, discum adeptus, vehementer ēmīsit.
discus longē per aurās volāvit et percussit...Sīlānum! cum lēgātus in terrā
exanimātus iacēret, Strȳthiō, ad Modestum versus,   20

"mī amīce," inquit, "nōs nōn iam oportet discum exercēre. nunc
oportet cursum exercēre! nōbīs quam celerrimē fugiendum est!"

duo mīlitēs statim exiērunt.

ōmīsit: ōmittere *drop, let fall*	**certant: certāre** *compete*
lūdī Olympicī *Olympic Games*	**mīlitant: mīlitāre** *serve in the army*
fīunt *are taking place*	**aggressus** *having attacked*
exercēbat: exercēre *practice*	**versus** *having turned*
palmam: palma *prize*	**nōn iam** *no longer*
caudicēs: caudex *blockhead, idiot*	**cursum: cursus** *racing, running*

Questions

1   What were the two soldiers doing when Silanus caught sight of them?
2   What complaint did he make to them?
3   What explanation did Strythio make for their actions?
4   What two criticisms did Silanus make about the soldiers' plans?
5   What crisis developed while this conversation was going on?
6   How did Modestus' efforts to be a hero work out?
7   What new sport did the two soldiers have to take up as a result?

I

Translate the following story.

mediā nocte iuvenis ad urbem Rōmam maximā cum dīligentiā
ambulābat. equus amīcīque in tabernā proximā relictī erant, ut iuvenis
sōlus urbī appropinquāre posset. subitō, cum sepulcra praeterīret,
hominem prope sepulcrum magnum stantem cōnspexit. iuvenis
cōnsistere coāctus est.   5

    "mihi cavendum est," sibi inquit. "nisi dēcipior, hic vir amōre
sepulcrōrum nimis afficitur. mē oportet tālēs virōs vītāre."
    deinde locum quaerēbat ubi sē cēlāret, unde hominem clam spectāret.
nam cognōscere voluit quid ille ibi faceret.
    subitō vir, iuvenem cōnspicātus, attonitus clāmāvit,   10
    "quis es? quis tē mīsit? cūr spectābar?"

praeterīret: praeterīre *go past*   **nisi** *unless*
cavendum: cavēre *beware*   **clam** *secretly*

II

Read the rest of the story and answer the questions which follow.

"advena sum," inquit iuvenis, "quī urbem Rōmam numquam anteā
vīsitāvī. tibi nocēre nōlō. tamen dīc mihi! cūr hīs sepulcrīs trāheris? num
umbrās quaeris?"
    "minimē," respondit alter. "quondam autem umbra mea hīc
habitātūra est. ego sum Quīntus Haterius Latrōniānus, redēmptor   5
nōtissimus. fortasse aedificia mea vīdistī: amphitheātrum Flāvium, arcum
novum...sed advena es! tū haec aedificia sānē nōn vīdistī. necesse est mihi
ea tibi...māne...ostendere! sed intereā, spectā haec sepulcra! nōnne
pulcherrima sunt?"
    iuvenis, quī nesciēbat num cum redēmptōre quī sepulcra amāret   10
dīcere vellet, nihilōminus assēnsit.
    "patrōnus," inquit Haterius, "mihi hunc agellum vēndidit, ubi
sepulcra mihi meīsque exstruerem. hīc nōmen meum aedificiaque mea in
sepulcrō sculpere in animō habeō et sīc facta mea dēclārāre. nōnne
patrōnus vir līberālis est?"   15
    "quot sestertiōs patrōnō dedistī ubi hic agellus vēnditus est?" rogāvit
iuvenis.
    "sestertium tantum trīciēns," respondit Haterius.
    "dī immortālēs!" clāmāvit iuvenis. "patrōnus tuus est fūr! sed amīcī
mē monuērunt nē quid Rōmae emerem. in oppidō Pompēiīs..."   20

"tūne Pompēiānus es?" clāmāvit redēmptor. "mercātōrem Pompēiānum cognōveram, nōmine Lūcium Caecilium Iūcundum."

"fīlius eius sum," respondit iuvenis, "Quīntus Caecilius Iūcundus. necesse est mihi..."

"necesse est tibi apud mē manēre," respondit Haterius. "et crās tibi aedificia mea et patrōnum meum ostendere volō!"

25

advena *stranger*
trāheris: trāhere *attract*
hīc *here*
habitātūra: habitātūrus *going to live*
redēmptor *builder, contractor*
arcum: arcus *arch*
nihilōminus *nevertheless*
assēnsit: assentīre *agree*
agellum: agellus *small plot of land*

sculpere *sculpt, carve*
in animō habeō: in animō habēre *intend, have in mind*
facta: factum *deed*
dēclārāre *make known*
sestertiōs: sestertius *sesterce*
trīciēns *three million*
nē quid *that...nothing; that not...anything*

Questions

1 According to his first question, what puzzled the young man most about the other man's behavior?

2 How did the other man (Haterius) first explain his fascination for the site?

3 What did Haterius promise he would do for the young man the next day?

4 What worry did the young man express to himself following this first part of the conversation?

5 What plans did Haterius have for this site?

6 How had he obtained the site?

7 What was the young man's reaction to the purchase price?

8 What offer did Haterius make when he discovered who the young man was?

9 Suggest why he made this offer.

10 Why would Quintus find it awkward to accept Haterius' last wish?

Haterius grātiās agit

I

Translate the following story.

Quīntus Haterius Latrōniānus, gaudiō commōtus, uxōrem in vīllā
quaerēbat. nam nūntius ad vīllam missus erat quī redēmptōrem ad aulam
Imperātōris invītāret. Haterius ā Domitiānō rogātus erat ut templum Iovis
Capitōlīnī reficeret. epistulam ab Imperātōre scrīptam manū tenēbat.
"nōs hodiē ob arcum magnificum honōrāmur," sibi inquit.   5
"Domitiānus arcū sānē dēlectātus est."
deinde, Vitelliam cōnspicātus, tōtam rem explicāvit. illa respondit:
"tē decet Salviō grātiās maximās agere, quod tantum opus, tanta
dignitās, tantae dīvitiae tibi datae sunt!"

gaudiō: gaudium *joy*
redēmptōrem: redēmptor *builder,*
contractor
Iovis Capitōlīnī: Iuppiter Capitōlīnus
Capitoline Jupiter (Jupiter as
worshiped on the Capitoline Hill)

reficeret: reficere *repair*
ob *because of*
arcum: arcus *arch*
magnificum: magnificus *magnificent*
honōrāmur: honōrāre *honor*

II

Read the rest of the story and answer the questions at the end.

illā nocte, Haterius in cubiculō graviter dormiēbat. in somniō templum
novum aedificābātur; columnae ingentēs, marmore factae, exstruēbantur;
tēctum aurātum in summō templō pōnēbātur. Imperātor, Salvius, plūrimī
senātōrēs vēnerant quī magnum opus laudārent. Domitiānus Hateriō
appropinquāvit ut eī nūntiāret: 5
"Quīnte Haterī Latrōniāne, tū sacerdōs iussū Imperātōris hodiē
creāris."
cum Haterius haec verba cōgitāret, subitō terra tremere coepit.
ingentēs marmoris massae ad terram dēcidēbant. multī senātōrēs hīs
massīs occīdēbantur; clāmōrēs cēterōrum ad caelum tollēbantur. Haterius 10
ibi stābat immōtus. subitō vōx dīra audīta est:

33

"vae tē, Haterī! Imperātōrī Salviōque grātiās ēgistī; tamen eum neglēxistī cuius templum exstruis. tē nōn oportet Iovem Optimum Maximum neglegere. cavē! cavē!..."

Haterius subitō excitātus est. pavōre commōtus, ad templum Iovis mediā nocte contendit et, deum precātus, sacrificium fēcit. 15

somniō: somnium *dream*
columnae: columna *column*
marmore: marmor *marble*
tēctum *roof*
aurātum: aurātus *gilded*
iussū: iussus *order*

tremere *shake, tremble*
massae: massa *block*
vae tē *alas for you*
neglēxistī: neglegere *overlook, ignore*
cuius *whose*
cavē: cavēre *beware*

Questions

1 What were two pleasant details of the scene Haterius saw in the first part of his dream?
2 What good news did the emperor deliver?
3 What were two unpleasant details of the scene Haterius saw in the last part of the dream?
4 What warning came from the voice in his dream?
5 What did Haterius do when he woke up?

30.3 # sacrificium

I

Translate the following story.

Gāius Salvius Līberālis cum paucīs amīcīs in fānō sacrō conveniēbat, quod in nemore prope urbem Rōmam exstrūctum erat. hī amīcī, quī sacerdōtēs Frātrum Arvālium ab Imperātōre creātī erant, sacrificia hōrā prīmā lūcis facere solēbant. itaque spē favōris Domitiānī commōtī, inter sē cōnsulēbant dē sacrificiō prō salūte Imperātōris. 5

"comitēs!" inquit Salvius. "Imperātor ab inimīcīs circumvenitur. nōs ob fidēlitātem iustē laudāmur. nōs igitur decet, quī hīs sacrificiīs praefectī sumus, victimam ēligere."

fānō: fānum *shrine*
nemore: nemus *grove*
Frātrum Arvālium: Frātrēs Arvālēs
  *Arval Brothers (a group of priests
  entrusted with the worship of the
  Emperor)*

favōris: favor *favor, support*
ob *because of*
fidēlitātem: fidēlitās *loyalty,
  trustworthiness*
iustē *rightly, justly*
victimam: victima *victim*

II

Read the rest of the story and answer the questions at the end.

postrīdiē haec victima, vacca alba, per viās Urbis ā servīs dūcēbātur.
subitō rēs dīra accidit. nam puella, quae ā tribus puerīs agitābātur, in
mediam viam irrūpit. illa, perīculī īnscia, servōs vaccamque nōn vīdit
neque illī eam; sub pedem vaccae ēlāpsa, graviter vulnerāta est. dolōre
paene exanimāta, tantā vōce clāmāvit ut multitūdō cīvium, strepitū   5
attracta, ad hanc viae partem festīnāret. soror puellae, pavōre dolōreque
eius affecta, aderat quae eam adiuvāret.
    "quamquam dolēs et terrēris," inquit, "tē oportet fortem esse. nōlī
dēspērāre! nōlī perīre!"
    interim Salvius, quī ante pompam incēdēbat neque vīderat quid   10
accidisset, cum clāmōrēs audīvisset, ad eōs contendit; ibi puellam
sorōremque in viā iacentēs, turbamque circumstantem cōnspexit.
postquam servī dē puellā nārrāvērunt, Salvius gladium dēstrīnxit eamque
trānsfīxit.
    "haec puella deōs offendit; itaque eī pereundum est," explicāvit ille.   15
    deinde cum servīs et vaccā ēgressus, turbam attonitam in viā stantem
relīquit.

vacca *cow*	**attracta: attractus** *attracted*
alba: albus *white*	**circumstantem: circumstāre** *stand around*
īnscia: īnscius *unaware*	**dēstrīnxit: dēstringere** *draw*
ēlāpsa: ēlāpsus *having slipped*	**trānsfīxit: trānsfīgere** *stab*

Questions

1 **rēs dīra accidit.** Describe the accident, giving three details.
2 Why did the accident attract a crowd?
3 What was the girl's sister doing?
4 Where was Salvius at this time?
5 What was his first indication that something was wrong?
6 What action did he take when he arrived on the scene and heard the
   story?
7 How did he explain his action?

30.4 sorōrēs Haterium monent

I

Translate the following story.

Rūfilla, uxor Salviī, in hortō sedēbat. subitō Vitellia, uxor Hateriī et soror
Rūfillae, in hortum ā servō ducta est. Rūfilla tam laeta erat cum Vitelliam
vīdisset ut, sorōrem amplexa, rogāret ut prope sē cōnsīderet. deinde
servus in vīllam missus est quī pōcula vīnī ferret.

"adventū tuō maximē dēlector, mea Vitellia," inquit Rūfilla. "nōs   5
oportet, quod ā marītīs semper dēserimur, inter nōs saepius vīsitāre.
valetne Haterius?"

"marītus meus vir minimae prūdentiae est," respondit Vitellia. "ubi
arcus Titī exstruēbātur, nimis labōrābat, spē favōris Domitiānī. nunc
dolōre īrāque afficitur, quod Imperātor ipse grātiās eī nōn ēgit. mē taedet   10
eius querēlārum."

cōnsīderet: cōnsīdere *sit down*   **favōris: favor** *favor, support*
valet: valēre *be well*   **querēlārum: querēla** *complaint*

II

Read the rest of the story and answer the questions at the end.

postquam Vitellia marītum sīc vituperāvit, duae fēminae inter sē
cōgitābant quō modō Haterium monēre possent. nam perīculōsum erat
Imperātōrem Domitiānum reprehendere. Vitellia igitur, metū commōta,
sorōrem vīsitāre coācta erat ut auxilium peteret.

    subitō Rūfilla rogāvit ubi esset Haterius eō tempōre.   5

    "ille in āreā cum fabrīs labōrat," respondit Vitellia. "cūr rogās?"

    "necesse est nōbīs nūntium ad āream mittere," inquit Rūfilla. "hic
servus Hateriō epistulam trādere potest, sīc scrīptam..." et Rūfilla verba
compōnere coepit:

    "cavē, Haterī! Imperātōrī placet praemium meritum eīs dare quōs   10
amat...et quōs ōdit. nōlī Imperātōrem offendere!"

    haec epistula, celeriter scrīpta, servō dāta est, quam ad Haterium
ferret. servus, quī certior nōn factum erat quid epistula monēret neque
quis eam scrīpsisset, ad āream contendit ut Haterium invenīret. mediā in
āreā eum cōnspexit, fabrōs incitantem...et dē Imperātōre mussitantem.   15
cum autem epistulam lēgisset, statim palluit et in massam marmoris lentē
cōnsēdit...

    posteā apud Haterium nihil plūs dē Imperātōre dictum est!

perīculōsum: perīculōsus *dangerous*
reprehendere *criticize*
āreā: ārea *building site*
compōnere *compose, put together*
meritum: meritus *well-deserved*
offendere *offend*

certior factum erat: certior facere
  inform
mussitantem: mussitāre *grumble,*
  mutter (to oneself)
massam: massa *block*
marmoris: marmor *marble*

Questions

1 Why did the two women feel it was necessary to warn Haterius about
    the way he was behaving?
2 Where did Rufilla suggest they send the warning message?
3 By either translating this message or paraphrasing it in your own
    words, explain how Rufilla decided to word their warning.
4 To make the warning as effective as possible, what did the women not
    tell the messenger slave about it?
5 What was Haterius doing when the slave found him?
6 What was his reaction to the letter?
7 How do we know that the warning had the effect the two women
    desired?

31.1 urbs barbarōrum

I

Translate the following story.

Euphrosynē et servus, postquam domō Hateriī abāctī sunt, per viās Urbis
prōcēdēbant ut locum invenīrent ubi habitārent. servus, quamquam
monitus erat nē dēspērāret, in animō volvēbat quārē ad hanc urbem
inimīcam vēnissent. ubīque enim, cum dēversōrium petīvissent, ā
dominīs superbīs spernēbantur. tandem servus, nūllō locō aptō inventō,   5
    "domina," inquit, "nōbīs ab hāc urbe discēdendum est. nam hīc nōs
dērīdēmur, ego in lūtum iacior, tū contumēliīs salutāris. Rōma urbs est
barbarōrum!"
    servus, hīs verbīs dictīs, sarcinās in umerōs sustulit ut ad portum
redīret.   *10*

abāctī sunt: abigere *drive away*	**hīc** *here*
dēversōrium: dēversōrium *lodgings,*	**lūtum: lūtum** *mud*
place to stay	**contumēliīs: contumēlia** *insult*
aptō: aptus *suitable*	**sarcinās: sarcinae** *bags, luggage*

II

Read the rest of the story and answer the questions at the end.

difficile autem erat ad portum contendere, turbā ingentī, quae eīs
obstābat, viās complente. haec multitūdō tōta in eandem partem
festīnābat. Euphrosynē, hīs rēbus animadversīs, servum rogāvit quō hī
Rōmānī contenderent. ille, clāmōre cīvium quoque attonitus, mercātōrī
praetereuntī clāmāvit,   5
    "amīce! quō festīnat haec multitūdō?"
    "nōnne scīs?" respondit alter. "hodiē Imperātor lūdōs magnificōs
nūntiāvit. nōs omnēs ad amphitheātrum novum contendimus, ubi
spectāculum optimum ēditur."
    tum per viās currere perrēxit.   *10*
    Euphrosynē, dubiō commōta, haec verba intellegere nōn poterat. nam
neque dē amphitheātrō audīverat neque spectācula ūlla vīderat. necesse
igitur erat servō haec explicāre:
    "in amphitheātrō pugnant gladiātōrēs, virī armātī, quī bēstiās,
captīvōs, aliōs gladiātōrēs occīdere temptant. gladiātōribus vincentibus   *15*
dantur glōria, pecūnia, etiam lībertās; gladiātōribus victīs dātur mors!"
    Euphrosynē, hīs verbīs attonita, pallēscēbat.
    "num cīvēs Rōmānī ad caedem festīnant?" rogāvit. "num virōs aliōs
virōs necantēs spectāre cupiunt?"

38

"ita vērō," respondit servus. *20*
Euphrosynē, hīs verbīs audītīs, clāmāvit,
"Rōma urbs est barbarōrum!"
tum sarcinās in umerōs servī sustulit et ad portum contendit.

partem: pars *direction*
animadversīs: animadvertere *notice*
magnificōs: magnificus *magnificent*
ēditur: ēdere *present, put on*
perrēxit: pergere *continue*
ūlla: ūllus *any*

armātī: armāre *arm*
bēstiās: bēstiae *animals, beasts*
glōria *fame, glory*
lībertās *freedom*
caedem: caedēs *slaughter, murder*

Questions

1 What difficulty did Euphrosyne and her slave encounter?
2 What was unusual about this situation?
3 How did the slave try to find out what was going on?
4 What information was he given?
5 Why did he have to give a further explanation to Euphrosyne?
6 What explanation did he give?
7 What could she not accept about this explanation?
8 What opinion of Rome did she form?

Tiberis flūmen

I

Translate the following story.

nox erat. prope urbem Rōmam iuvenis, paucīs servīs comitantibus, per
Viam Flāminiam equitābat. lentē prōgrediēbātur nē cīvēs quī prope viam
habitābant excitāret. servī quoque monitī erant ut summā dīligentiā
prōcēderent. quī igitur, silvās, agrōs, etiam praetereuntēs perscrūtātī,
dominum sequēbantur.   5
    tandem ad Pontem Mulvium pervēnērunt, ubi iuvenis, quamquam
itinere vigiliāque fessus erat, tacitē rīdēbat.
    "nunc urbem Rōmam ingredior," sibi cōgitāvit, "ubi habitat Gāius
Salvius Līberālis, quī mihi pūniendus est...et quem pūnītūrus sum!"

Tiberis *Tiber (the river flowing through Rome)*
comitantibus: comitāns *accompanying*
Viam Flāminiam: Via Flāminia *the Via Flaminia (the main road going north
    from Rome)*
equitābat: equitāre *ride*
perscrūtātī: perscrūtātus *having examined (closely)*
Pontem Mulvium: Pōns Mulvius *the Mulvian Bridge (where the Via Flaminia
    crosses the Tiber River)*
vigiliā: vigilia *lack of sleep*

II

Read the rest of the story and answer the questions at the end.

hic iuvenis erat Quīntus Caecilius Iūcundus. quī, ē Britanniā post mortem
Cogidubnī summā celeritāte ēgressus, decem mēnsēs multās per terrās
errāverat. nam metū Salviī affectus, Rōmam rēctē petere non ausus erat.
nunc tandem, multa perīcula passus, ad Urbem ipsam pervēnerat.
    tam laetō animō erat cum dē adventū suō cōgitāret ut ad mediam   5
pontem prōgressus, subitō in flūmen sē coniceret. servī, quī dominum
natantem attonitī spectābant, omnīnō nesciēbant cūr hoc faceret. ille
tamen, eōs attonitōs cōnspicātus, clāmāvit,
    "nōlīte anxiī esse, mī comitēs! hoc flūmen nōtissimum per urbem
Rōmam fluit. in hoc flūmen cīvēs īrātī statuās inimīcōrum saepe abiciunt.   10
in hoc flūmen aliquandō inimīcōs ipsōs abiciunt!
    "ego Salvium tālem inimīcum putō. aliīs Rōmānīs de sceleribus eius
dīcere volō. quondam hī cīvēs Salviī statuam, aut Salvium ipsum, in
Tiberim iactūrī sunt. ego meā sponte in flūmine natō; quō factō, Salviō dē
aquae frīgore monēre possum!"   15

40

mēnsēs: mēnsis *month*
rectē *straight*
natantem: natāre *swim*

putō: putāre *consider*
meā sponte *of my own will*
frīgore: frīgus *coldness, coolness*

Questions

1 How long had it taken Quintus to get to Rome from Britain?
2 Why had it taken him so long?
3 What strange action did he take, in his happiness at reaching Rome?
4 What effect did his action have on his slaves?
5 What Roman custom did Quintus refer to, regarding the Tiber River?
6 What hope did he express about Salvius' future?
7 How did Quintus explain his present strange actions in connection with that future hope?

somnium explicātum

I

Translate the following story.

nox erat. Quīntus Haterius Latrōniānus anxius in hortō ambulābat. nam
rēs dīra in somniō vīsa eum adeō terruerat ut dormīre nōn posset. mediā
nocte ē cubiculō ēgressus erat ut rem cōgitāret, sed quid sibi faciendum
esset omnīnō nesciēbat.

    Vitellia, dum Haterius paulīsper in sellā sedet, virō cōgitantī   5
appropinquāvit. Hateriō enim ē vīllā ēgressō, illa cognōscere cōnstituerat
quō īret, cūr dormīre nōn posset, quid deinde factūrus esset.

    Haterius, uxōre vīsā, sollicitūdinem cēlāre cōnābātur. illa tamen verbīs
mollibus eī persuāsit ut tōtam rem nārrāret. quō factō, Haterius aequiōre
animō in vīllam regressus est.   10

sollicitūdinem: sollicitūdō   mollibus: mollis *soft, gentle*
   worry, anxiety

II

Read the rest of the story and answer the questions at the end.

posterō diē Vitellia marītō dē somniō sīc locūta est:
    "tibi ad Salvium eundum est. nam philosophus Athēnodōrus, amīcus
eius, somnia intellegit. hic philosophus somnium tuum audītum tibi
explicāre potest."

    Haterius, hīs verbīs uxōris adductus, ad Salvium prōfectus est. quī   5
forte vīsitābātur ab Athēnodōrō, cui Haterius somnium sīc nārrāvit:
    "in somniō, Imperātor Domitiānus mihi imperāvit ut aulam
magnificam aedificārem. itaque ego summā celeritāte Imperātōrī pāruī.
sed aula quae tam celeriter exstructa erat tantā celeritāte dēlēta est. unā

42

nocte mūrī, tēctum, tōta aula humum prōcubuērunt! ab Imperātōre
vituperātus sum; ad carcerem ductus sum, ubi custōdēs mē interfectūrī
erant. subitō excitātus sum. nunc sollicitūdinem meam intellegere potes?"

Athēnodōrus autem vōce compositā respondit:

"nōnnūllī somnia habent quae rem contrāriam significant. nōlī anxius
esse. tibi prōmittō aulam magnificam, praemium magnum ab Imperātōre
datum...et vītam longam!"

Haterius animō levātō ad vīllam regressus est.

philosophus *philosopher*	**compositā: compositus** *steady,*
magnificam: magnificus	*composed*
magnificent	**rem contrāriam: rēs contrāria** *the opposite*
tēctum *roof*	**significant: significāre** *mean, indicate*
humum *to the ground*	**levātō: levāre** *lighten, relieve*
prōcubuērunt: prōcumbere *fall down*	

Questions

1 Why did Vitellia suggest that Haterius go to Salvius?
2 What happy coincidence happened when Haterius arrived at Salvius'
   house?
3 In Haterius' dream, what request did the emperor make?
4 What happened to Haterius' work?
5 What sentence did the emperor impose?
6 How did Athenodorus interpret the dream for Haterius?
7 How did Haterius react to that interpretation?

32.3   ultiō Hateriī

I

Translate the following story.

post cēnam turbulentam, Eryllus, Hateriī arbiter ēlegantiae, valdē
timēbat. nam triclīniō ā convīvīs dēlētō, philosophāque ad Graeciam
regressā, in animō volvēbat num Haterius sē dīmissūrus esset.

"dominus mihi vītandus est," sibi cōgitāvit. "cōnsilium novum
invenīre cōgor."

Eryllō haec cōgitante, Haterius ipse per iānuam irrūpit, valdē
permōtus. quī, quamquam Eryllus īram eius lēnīre cōnābātur, effūsīsque
lacrimīs ōrābat nē sē pūnīret, hīs verbīs nōn affectus est.

turbulentam: turbulentus *rowdy*	**convīvīs: convīva** *guest*
arbiter *judge*	**lēnīre** *soothe, calm*
ēlegantiae: ēlegantia *good taste*	

43

II

Read the rest of the story and answer the questions at the end.

"caudex!" clāmāvit patrōnus īrātus. "tuō beneficiō lūdibrium Rōmae nunc
sum. Sabīnus, cōnsul summae auctōritātis cuius favōrem conciliāre
cōnābar, mē nunc dēspicit. quō modō ad summōs honōrēs pervenīre
possum, cōnsule mē dēspiciente? ā clientibus, quī ad cēnam invītātī sunt,
nunc dērīdeor. quō modō favōrem populī Rōmānī conciliāre possum,   5
clientibus mē ad forum dēdūcere nōlentibus? triclīnium in quō
cēnābāmus tōtum dīreptum est. quō modō clientēs novōs invenīre
possum, sī eōs ad cēnam invītāre prohibeor?

   "cūr tū petauristāriōs nōn condūxistī? petauristāriī convīvās nōn
castīgant. petauristāriī convīvās ad pugnam nōn incitant. petauristāriī   10
omnēs Rōmānōs dēlectant!

   "sed poenam aptissimam sciō! tū philosophās Graecās amās? tū
urbem Athēnās laudās? optimē! tibi ad urbem Athēnās statim
proficīscendum est, unde tē numquam redīre volō. abī!"

caudex: **caudex** *blockhead, idiot*
tuō beneficiō *thanks to you*
lūdibrium *laughing-stock*
favōrem: **favor** *favor, support*
conciliāre *win over*
dēspicit: **dēspicere** *look down on, despise*
dēdūcere *escort*
dīreptum est: **dīripere** *ransack, tear apart*
prohibeor: **prohibēre** *prevent*
petauristāriōs: **petauristārius** *acrobat*
aptissimam: **aptus** *suitable*

Questions

1   In the first paragraph of his speech, Haterius indicates three problems
    that have arisen because of the ill-fated banquet, and he also indicates
    the reasons for these problems. In your own words, summarize these
    problems and their causes, as Haterius sees them.
2   What are three reasons he gives for feeling that acrobats would have
    been a better choice of entertainment?
3   What appropriate punishment has Haterius decided on for Eryllus?
4   Why does he feel it is appropriate?

44

poena Hateriī

I

Translate the following story.

media nox erat. omnibus convīvīs domum regressīs, Haterius in triclīniō
sōlus sedēbat, in animō volvēns quid factūrus esset. nam convīvīs
pugnantibus, triclīnium paene dēlētum erat. cōnsul Sabīnus, cum ē vīllā
exīret, Hateriō imperāverat nē sē ad cēnam iterum invītāret. Euphrosynē
tamen, hīs rēbus vīsīs, vultū serēnō ēgressa erat ut ad portum redīret.   5

   "illa philosopha," sibi cōgitāvit Haterius, "quae omnia haec effēcit,
mihi pūnienda est."

convīvīs: convīva *guest*　　　　　　**effēcit: efficere** *cause*

II

Read the rest of the story and answer the questions at the end.

diē illūcēscente, Haterius ad flūmen Tiberim summā celeritāte profectus
est, ut Euphrosynēn invenīret. redēmptor, cum per viās contenderet,
philosopham omnēsque Graecōs vituperābat:

   "Graecī sunt hominēs inūtilissimī: numquam enim labōrant; semper
cōgitant. deinde, quod dē sententiīs suīs cōnsentīre nōn possunt, inter sē   5
semper pugnant. nunc ad urbem nostram veniunt, hās sententiās
rīdiculās ferentēs...et nunc Rōmānī inter sē quoque pugnant. ego illam
philosopham comprehēnsūrus et ad iūdicem tractūrus sum, quia
triclīnium meum dēlēvit."

   cum ad portum vēnisset, statim in nāvem cōnscendit ut Euphrosynēn   10
summā dīligentiā quaereret. subitō puellam ad cavernam dēscendentem
cōnspicātus,

   "scelesta!" magnā vōce appellāvit Haterius. "cūr ex urbe ēgrederis?
tibi mēcum redeundum est! tē oportet poenās dare, quod domum meam
dēlēvistī."   15

   puella, clāmōre audītō, ad Haterium conversa, aequō animō cum eō
redīre parāvit. subitō, tamen, ambō nāvem sē moventem sēnsērunt.

   "heus!" clāmāvit Haterius. "mihi ē nāvī dēscendendum est!"

   redēmptor perterritus per nāvem quam celerrimē currere coepit.
deinde, postquam ad extrēmam nāvis partem advēnit, magnō clāmōre in   20
flūmen dēsiluit. ibi strēnuē iactābātur, Euphrosynēn omnēsque
philosophōs vituperāns.

illūcēscente: illūcēscere *dawn,
    grow bright*
celeritāte: celeritās *swiftness, speed*
redēmptor *contractor, builder*
inūtilissimī: inūtilis *useless*
rīdiculās: rīdiculus *silly*

cavernam: caverna *hold (of a ship)*
heus! *hey!*
extrēmam partem: extrēma pars *end,
    back, stern*
dēsiluit: dēsilīre *jump down*
iactābātur *was thrashing about*

Questions

1 What did Haterius do the next day?
2 What mood was he in?
3 Indicate two reasons he gave himself for disliking Greeks.
4 What were his intentions if he found Euphrosyne?
5 Where did he catch up to her?
6 How did she respond when he called her?
7 What emergency suddenly arose for Haterius?
8 What was the last picture Euphrosyne had of him?

34.1   aedificium novum

I

Translate the following story.

Salvius, ad vīllam rūsticam regressus, cum uxōre, Rūfillā, loquī voluit.
quam in hortō invēnit, Haterium Vitelliamque exspectantem.

"nūntium optimum ferō!" clāmāvit. "Paride occīsō Domitiāque
relēgātā, Imperātor mihi cōnsulātum prōmīsit. tamen dē Hateriō et sorōre
tuā sollicitus sum, quī apud nōs adhūc manent. illī, sī ad Urbem redierint,   5
domum ā pantomīmō incēnsam, ā mīlitibus dīreptam vidēbunt. quae
duōbus mēnsibus reficiētur. quō modō eōs vērum cognōscere
prohibēbimus?"

rūsticam: rūsticus *(in the) country*
nūntium: nūntius *news*
relēgātā: relēgāre *exile*
cōnsulātum: cōnsulātus *consulship*

pantomīmō: pantomīmus *actor*
dīreptam: dīripere *ransack*
mēnsibus: mēnsis *month*
prohibēbimus: prohibēre *prevent*

II

Read the rest of the story and answer the questions at the end.

Salviō Rūfillāque dē hīs rēbus paulīsper locūtīs, reversī sunt Haterius et
Vitellia, quī per silvās prope mare ambulāverant. eīs in hortum
ingredientibus obviam iit Salvius ut laetissimē salutāret.

"fēlicissimī sumus," clāmāvit. "Imperātor, quod mē auctōre Domitia
cum Paride capī poterat, mihi cōnsulātum prōmīsit. tū quoque, mī Haterī,   5
praemiō honōrāberis."

Haterius, gaudiō permōtus, vix dīcere poterat. tandem patrōnum
rogāvit quāle praemium Domitiānus ēlēgisset.

"Imperātor," respondit Salvius, "quod uxōris perfidae oblīvīscī vult,
aulam novam aedificāre cōnstituit. īnsulam Capreās, ubi prīnceps   10
Tiberius multōs annōs habitābat, īnspicere cupit. placetne tibi ad hanc
īnsulam nāvigāre, ibi per duōs mēnsēs manēre, locum idōneum ēligere,
dēscrīptiōnēs facere? tibi licēbit Vitelliam tēcum dūcere."

Haterius et Vitellia haec verba vix crēdere poterant. Vitellia quidem
Salviō rogāvit,   15

"nōnne iocāris?"

Salvius tamen aequō animō respondit,

"vērum dīcō. propter cōnsilia mea, Imperātor ipse 'aedificium
novum,' inquit, 'praemium idōneum Hateriō erit.'"

oblīvīscī *forget (+ genitive case)*
Capreās: Capreae *Capri (an island
    near Naples)*
idōneum: idōneus *suitable*
dēscrīptiōnēs: dēscrīptiō *plan, drawing*

tibi licēbit: tibi licet *you may, you
    are permitted/allowed*
quidem *indeed*
iocāris: iocārī *joke, be joking*
propter *because of*

Questions

1 Salvius and Rufilla had concocted quite a story for Haterius and his wife:
  a What, supposedly, did the emperor want to do?
  b Why did he want to do this?
  c How did Salvius explain the emperor's choice of location?
  d What instructions did Salvius have from the emperor for Haterius?
2 What was Vitellia's reaction to all of this?
3 Explain how Salvius' last assurance to Vitellia is true, in an ironic way.

34.2 cōnsilium pūmiliōnis

I

Translate the following story.

nocte appropinquante, iuvenis per viās Urbis celeriter prōgrediēbātur.
nam epistulā mīrābilī acceptā, ad flūmen Tiberim prōfectus erat ut auctōrī
obviam īret. cum pontem trānsīret, lūmen in tenebrīs cōnspicātus est.
  "Quīntus Caecilius Iūcundus?" rogāvit vōx.
  Quīntus nihil respondit. in animō tamen volvit,   5
  "quid factūrus sum, sī hic mē necāre temptāverit?"
  subitō pūmiliō ā tenebrīs appāruit, Quīntumque sē sequī iussit. ille,
īnsidiās suspicātus, recūsāvit. pūmiliō igitur, nē iuvenem terrēret, haec
verba aequō animō loquī coepit:
  "Myropnous sum, amīcus Paridis, pantomīmī quī Gāiō Salviō auctōre   10
occīsus est. nōnne īdem Salvius, cum in Britanniam pervēnisset, rēgem
Cogidubnum, amīcum tuum, occīdī iussit? sī mē adiūveris, ultiōnem
idōneam parāre poterimus. sī mihi
crēdideris, Salvius mox pūniētur...et
ego tībiīs iterum cantābō."

pūmiliōnis: pūmiliō *dwarf*
lūmen: lūmen *light*
pantomīmī: pantomīmus *actor*
idōneam: idōneus *suitable*
tībiīs: tībia *pipe*

II

Read the rest of the story and answer the questions at the end.

Quīntus, hīs verbīs audītīs, rīdēre coepit. nam Paride mortuō Domitiāque
relēgātā, rūmōrēs per tōtam Urbem vulgātī erant. aliī Epaphrodītum
suspicātī erant, aliī Imperātōrem ipsum. nēmō tamen nōmen Salviī
commemorāverat. Quīntus autem, quī hunc senātōrem bene cognōverat,
verba Myropnoī facile crēdere poterat.   5

"mī amīce," inquit, "tibi cōnfīdere possum, et tū mihi! Salvius mihi
odiō summō est, quia in Britanniā nōn sōlum rēgem fidēlissimum sed
etiam mē ipsum interficere cōnātus, Agricolam, lēgātum Rōmānum, dē
hīs rēbus dēcipere temptāvit. sed nōbīs cavendum est, quod Salvius
summam potestātem apud Imperātōrem habet."   10

"multī virī summae potestātis ab Imperātōribus occīsī sunt," respondit
Myropnous. "Vespasiānus, pater Domitiānī, Helvidium Priscum,
senātōrem nōtissimum, interficī iussit, postquam dēlātōrēs dē sententiīs
Stōicīs Helvidiī nārrāvērunt. Domitiānus, magis quam pater, dēlātōrēs
excipere vult. Salvius, vir summae calliditātis, āctōrem rēgemque cōnsiliīs   15
audācibus occīdere cupiēbat. nōnne Imperātor ipse ab hōc virō callidō
quoque interficī potest? sī haec Domitiānō per dēlātōrēs quibus Imperātor
cōnfīdit nārrāverimus, ille Salvium mox suspicābitur, timēbit...et
removēbit! Imperātor nōbīs celeriter 'monendum' est."

quibus verbīs audītīs, Quīntus rīsit.   20
"mī amīce," inquit, "brevī tempore tū tībiīs iterum cantābis!"

relēgātā: relēgāre *exile*
rūmōrēs: rūmor *rumor*
vulgātī erant: vulgāre *spread*
cavendum: cavēre *beware*

dēlātōrēs: dēlātor *informer*
calliditātis: calliditās *cleverness*
removēbit: removēre *remove*
tībiīs: tībia *pipe*

Questions

1 What rumors had been flying around Rome after Paris' death and
   Domitia's exile?
2 Why was Quintus surprised to hear of Salvius' link with the story?
3 How did the mention of Salvius actually help Quintus to trust
   Myropnous?
4 What two items of information did Quintus add about Salvius' actions
   in Britain – information which Myropnous might not have known?
5 What concern did Quintus express about acting against Salvius?
6 What incident from the past did Myropnous mention to prove that
   senators were not immune to punishment?
7 Briefly outline the plan he had in mind to "frame" Salvius.
8 From the stories in our text, explain the reference in Quintus' last
   remark (and Myropnous' last remark in Part I).

I

Translate the following story.

Ceriālis, servus quī in aulā Imperātōris labōrābat, līberārī voluit. epistulīs
Domitiānī multōs per annōs scrīptīs, in animō volvēbat num prīnceps sibi
lībertātem umquam datūrus esset. tamen, quod ipse virum tantā
auctōritāte rogāre nōn audēbat, epistulam aliam scrībere ad
Imperātōremque mittere cōnstituit, et hōc modō lībertātem adipīscī.   5

"nōnne," sibi cōgitāvit servus, "sī Domitiānus verba mea lēgerit,
celeriter respondēbit? sī mihi lībertātem dederit, eī grātiae mihi agendae
erunt. sī recūsāverit, servus manēbō."

Ceriālis, hīs verbīs sibi dictīs, deōs precātus est nē Domitiānus
recūsāret.   10

II

Read the rest of the story and answer the questions at the end.

Titus Flāvius Ceriālis, lībertus Augustī, laetus per aulam Domitiānī
ambulābat. in manibus multās epistulās ab Imperātōre dictātās ferēbat. in
cubiculō tamen ūnam epistulam servābat, in quā prīnceps sibi lībertātem
prōmīserat. nam Domitiānus, epistulā Ceriālis acceptā, cōnsiliō audācī
dēlectātus, servum ipsum arcessīverat et epistulam Ceriālī dictāverat, eī   5
lībertātem offerēns. quam epistulam Ceriālis vītā suā custōdiēbat!

Ceriālis autem, postquam ā Domitiānō līberātus est, ancillam
pulcherrimam in aulā quondam cōnspicātus, adamāverat. haec ancilla,
Philaenis nōmine, ōrnātrīx Domitiae erat. quam cum vīdisset, Ceriālis
iterum sibi cōgitāverat,   10

"ēheu! quam pulchram puellam! lībertīs tamen ancillās in
mātrimōnium dūcere nōn licet. servī ancillās, sīcut 'coniugēs', tenēre
possunt. servus autem nōn sum! cūr lībertātem quaesīvī?

"...sed cōnsilium habeō. pecūniā servātā, aliam epistulam ad
Imperātōrem scrībam. sī ille mē passus erit, lībertātem Philaenīdis   15
ēmptūrus sum."

lībertus Augustī igitur laetus per
aulam Domitiānī ambulābat.

adamāverat: adamāre *fall in love with*
ōrnātrīx *hairdresser*
lībertīs licet *freedmen are allowed*
in mātrimōnium dūcere *marry*
coniugēs: coniunx *mate, spouse*
passus erit: patī *allow*

| D M |
| T. FLAVIVS CERIALIS |
| FLAVIAE PHILAENIDI |
| LIBERTAE IDEM |
| ET COIVGI |
| B M F |

50

Questions

1 How do we know, from the first sentence, that Cerialis has obtained the wish he expressed in the first part of this story?
2 How had the emperor reacted when he received Cerialis' request?
3 What 'joke' had the emperor played in return?
4 How do we know that Cerialis treasured the emperor's reply?
5 What complication had since arisen for Cerialis?
6 In his thoughts to himself, how did he find this situation ironic?
7 What plan did he come up with, which he hoped would eventually solve his problem?

34.4   multa mīrābilia

I

Translate the following story.

prīmā hōrā diēī, Quīntus Haterius Latrōniānus, cūrīs cōnfectus, prope flūmen Tiberim errābat. nam triclīniō ā convīvīs dīreptō, iānuāque flammīs paene dēlētā (dum Domitia Parisque effugere conantur), in animō volvēbat cūr deī sē pūnīrent. redēmptor, cum haec sibi cōgitāret, corpus sub ponte iacēns subitō cōnspicātus est.   5

"dī immortālēs!" sibi inquit Haterius. "Euphrosynē est, philosopha quam pūnītūrus eram. sī quis mē prope corpus invēnerit, ego in carcerem coniciar. quō modō hoc corpus hīc positum est? quis hoc fēcit? quid aliud mihi accidet?"

deinde "fortasse," sibi inquit, "corpus mihi in flūmen iaciendum est."   10

mīrābilia *strange things, amazing things*
cōnfectus *overcome*
convīvīs: convīva *guest*
dīreptō: dīripere *ransack*
redēmptor *contractor, builder*
sī quis *if anyone*

II

Read the rest of the story and answer the questions at the end.

Haterius, corpus ad flūminis rīpam tractūrus, trēs amīcōs pontī
appropinquantēs cōnspexit. celeriter sē sub pontem cēlāvit, in animō
volvēns num amīcī corpus vidēre possent. illī tamen, quod intentē inter sē
loquēbantur, pontem ignārī trānsiērunt.

"perīculōsum est," inquit sibi Haterius, "corpus ad flūmen trahī.   5
fortasse mihi quam celerrimē fugiendum est...sed sī quis mē ā ponte
currentem cōnspexerit, mē comprehendet. fortasse melius est per viās
lentē prōgredī quasi nihil mīrābile vīdissem."

Hateriō haec cōgitante, Gāius Salvius Līberālis pontī appropinquāvit.
quem cum vīdisset, Haterius,   10

"āctum est dē mē!" inquit. "nisi patrōnum meum vītāverim, sine
dubiō ille mē suspicābitur. quō fugiam?"

at Salvius, Hateriō...et corpore philosophae...vīsō, clientī imperāvit nē
fugeret. redēmptōrem miserum sīc grātulātus est:

"hanc puellam agnōscō, nōn sōlum pulchram sed perīculōsam. est   15
philosopha Stōica, inimīca Imperātōrī Domitiānō. ille tibi grātiās maximās
aget, cum dē morte eius audīverit. ad aulam nōbīs festīnandum est!"

et patrōnus clientem obstupefactum ad Imperātōrem dūxit.

perīculōsum: perīculōsus *dangerous*	**grātulātus est: grātulārī**
āctum est dē mē *it's all over for me*	*congratulate*
redēmptōrem: redēmptor *contractor, builder*	

Questions

1 What prevented Haterius from carrying out his first plan?
2 What second plan did Haterius think of?
3 What objection could he see to that second plan?
4 What third possible course of action did he come up with?
5 What prevented him from carrying that out?
6 At the end of the story, Haterius is described as **obstupefactum**.
   Briefly explain the reason for this state of mind.

titulī minantēs

I

Translate the following story.

Salvius, postquam cōnsul ab Imperātōre Domitiānō factus est, ad forum
cotīdiē īre solēbat. quondam, dum cūriam ingreditur, titulum novum in
mūrō scrīptum cōnspexit:

nūlla erit fuga!

cēterī senātōrēs, hōc titulō vīsō, inter sē rogābant quis haec verba
scrīpsisset atque quid significārent. Salvius tamen magnā vōce silentium   5
poposcit.
   "amīcī," clāmāvit, "hic titulus nōbīs dīligenter īnspiciendus est.
titulum eundem in aliīs aedificiīs tōtam per urbem iam vīdimus. quisquis
haec scrīpsit titulōs plūrēs scrīptūrus est. sī significātiōnem hōrum
verbōrum invēnerimus, cōnsilium capiēmus quō hic scelestus   10
comprehendī poterit. tum celeriter removēbitur!"
   Salviō hoc dīcente, senātōrēs rīdēre coeperant. ille autem eōs
hortābātur nē rīdērent priusquam auctōrem titulōrum pūnīvissent.

titulī: titulus *inscription, sign*   **quisquis** *whoever*
minantēs: minārī *threaten*   **significātiōnem: significātiō** *meaning*
cūriam: cūria *senate-house*   **removēbitur: removēre** *remove*
significārent: significāre *signify, mean*

II

Read the rest of the story and answer the questions at the end.

Salvius domum regressus uxōrī Rūfillae dē titulīs loquēbātur. dē
sententiīs senātōrum nihil dīxit quod nōn decet senātōrem cum uxōre dē
rēbus senātōriīs loquī. illa, cum verba titulōrum audīvisset: 'nūlla erit
fuga!', exclāmāvit,
   "soror mea, Vitellia, haec verba commemorāvit cum dē pantomīmō   5
Paride nārrāret. lībertus quīdam, scīlicet Chrīstiānus, amīcōs eius Paridem
laudantēs minātus est. pantomīmum monuit nē vitia sua pergeret, nisi ā
Deō pūnīrī vellet. 'flammās dē caelō missās' et 'nūllam fugam'
minābātur."
   "optimē!" clāmāvit Salvius. "quis erat hic lībertus? nōmen eius   10
commemorāvit Vitellia?"
   "Clītō...Tychlitō...oblīta sum," respondit uxor. "sed erat cliēns Titī
Flāviī Clēmentis. hoc meminī."

"ad Clēmentem igitur mihi festīnandum est," cachinnāvit Salvius. "mī
cārissime līberte, tū Deō ūnī crēdis? tū huic Deō grātiās agis, quod Paris   15
mortuus est? tū nōs senātōrēs minārī nunc audēs? tibi cavendum est. ego,
nōn Deus tuus, auctor erat exitiī Paridis. et ego auctor mortis tuae quoque
erō."

senātōriīs: senātōrius *senatorial, of the senate*
scīlicet *obviously*
vitia: vitium *sin*
pergeret: pergere *continue, go on with*
oblīta sum: oblīvīscī *forget*
meminī *I remember*
cachinnāvit: cachinnāre *laugh, chortle*
cavendum: cavēre *beware*

Questions

1 Why did Salvius not mention the discussion in the senate when
   talking to Rufilla about the wall signs?
2 Why did Rufilla recognize the message on the signs?
3 Give three details that Rufilla mentioned from the story we read in the
   textbook.
4 What other information was she able to give, to help her husband?
5 If the man we called Tychicus in our stories was indeed the guilty
   party, what line of thinking on Tychicus' part did Salvius suggest had
   led to the outbreak of signs?
6 What news and warning did Salvius have for the freedman?

36.1 poēta stultus

I

Translate the following story.

poēta Martiālis per urbem contendit amīcum vīsitātum. libellum novum
sēcum fert, quod bene scit hunc amīcum epigrammata mīrārī. per forum
trānsiēns, animadvertit magnam turbam prope rostra rīdēre atque
clāmāre.

"putō mē propius appropinquāre dēbēre," sibi inquit, "ut cognōscam
cur haec turba excitētur. suspicor enim aliquid rīdiculum accidere...et tū,   5
Martiālis, scīs tē rēbus rīdiculīs semper trahī."

libellum: libellus *booklet*   **rīdiculum: rīdiculus** *ridiculous, silly*
epigrammata: epigramma *epigram*   **trahī: trahere** *attract*
rostra: rostra *the Rostra (speaker's platform)*

II

Read the rest of the story and answer the questions at the end.

poēta, postquam propius appropinquāvit, senem in rostrīs stantem, dē
libellō recitātum, cōnspicātur. tamen, quotiēns recitātiōnis initium fēcit,
turba magnā vōce cachinnat. tandem, omnibus paulīsper tacentibus,
senex incipit:

       "dīcis amōre tuī bellās ardēre puellās,   5
          quī faciem sine aquā, Sexte, natantis habēs."

    prīmō audītōrēs nihil dīcunt, quod haec verba intellegere nōn possunt.
    "quō modō," inquit ūnus audītōrum, "Sextus sine aquā natāre potest?
hoc epigramma stultum est."
    tum audītōrēs senem vituperāre atque dērīdēre incipiunt.   10
    Martiālis, quī nunc īrāscitur, sibi dīcit:
    "hic senex tam stultus est ut epigrammata mea auferat neque verba
intellegat. Sextus *sub* aquā, nōn *sine* aquā natat. caudex!"
    dum Martiālis haec sibi cōgitat, senex aliud epigramma recitāre
cōnātur: 15

       "Thāida Quīntus amat. 'quam Thāida?' 'Thāida caecam.'
          nūllum oculum Thāis illa habet, ille duōs."

    Martiālis, quī sē continēre iam nōn potest, exclāmat:
    "satis! satis! hic asinus mea epigrammata dēlet! amīcī! hortor ut mē
audiātis."   20
    audītōrēs, quī Martiālem agnōscunt, tacent ut poēta loquātur. ille,
senem intentē spectāns, clāmat:
    "quis es, homuncule?"
    "Fīdentīnus sum," inquit senex, ērubēscēns.
    "tū male recitās, amīce," respondet Martiālis. "sed fortasse tū melius 25
recitāris. hoc audī!

       quem recitās meus est, ō Fīdentīne, libellus;
          sed male cum recitās, incipit esse tuus."

    Martiāle haec verba locūtō, audītōrēs rīdent, plaudunt, senem ē forō
agitant.   30

initium: initium *beginning*	**caudex: caudex** *blockhead, idiot*
cachinnat: cachinnāre *laugh, chortle*	**caecam: caecus** *blind*
bellās: bellus *pretty*	**continēre** *contain*
faciem: faciēs *face*	**homuncule: homunculus** *little man*
natantis: natāre *swim*	**ērubēscēns: ērubēscere** *blush*
prīmō *at first*	
audītōrēs: audītor *listener,*	
audience member	

Questions

1 What is Martial able to see when he gets closer?
2 How is the crowd behaving?
3 The first epigram is a copy of one of Martial's, but there is one mistake in it. What is that mistake? (Martial himself comments on it.)
4 Because of this error, what reaction does one listener have to the poem?
5 What is Martial's own comment about the poet?
6 Explain how the second epigram ruins Martial's original.
7 How does Martial react to this situation?
8 How does the crowd react? Why?
9 Translate the epigram Martial recites about Fidentinus.
10 How does the audience react to it?

36.2 dē poētā Martiāle

I

Translate the following story.

Martiālis hanc epistulam amīcō, Iuvenālī, scrīptum, in tablīnō sedet:
   "cum tū clāmōribus turbīsque Urbis vexārēris, ego ad patriam,
Hispāniam, revertēbar. scīsne mē ad tertiam hōram dormīre nunc posse?
crēdere potes vīcīnōs nōn hortārī ut togam semper geram? coquus, quī
intellegit mē in silvīs vēnātiōnem cupere, cibum tam bonum parat ut
bēstiārum saepe oblītus sim. mihi placēbit sīc vīvere, sīc perīre."   5

56

II

Read the rest of the story and answer the questions at the end.

Martiālis, ad Hispāniam reversus, paucīs annīs mortuus est. cuius post
mortem, Gāius Plīnius Secundus, scrīptor nōtissimus et Martiālis amīcus,
epistulam composuit, ingenium artemque poētae mortuī laudātum. hoc
fēcit, quod Martiālis epigramma Plīnium laudāns paucīs ante annīs
composuerat.   5
    crēdisne omnēs cīvēs Rōmānōs cum Plīniō assentīre? haec verba lege,
ut cōnstituās num Fabulla, fēmina vetus, assentiat:

>   omnēs aut vetulās habēs amīcās
>   aut turpēs vetulīsque foediōrēs;
>   hās dūcis comitēs trahisque tēcum   10
>   per convīvia, porticūs, theātra:
>   sīc formōsa Fabulla, sīc puella es.

    Laetīnus, senex, quoque putat amīcōs dēcipī posse. hōsne versūs
legere velit?

>   mentīris iuvenem tinctīs, Laetīne, capillīs,   15
>   tam subitō corvus, quī modo cȳcnus erās.
>   nōn omnēs fallis; scit tē Prōserpina cānum (esse):
>   persōnam capitī dētrahet illa tuō.

Martiālis quoque scrībit Linum, virum dīvitem, vīllam suam (quam "agrum" appellat) dērīdēre. Linus, quod saepe rogat cūr poēta in tam parvā vīllā maneat, hōc modō pūnītur: 20

> quid mihi reddat ager quaeris, Line, Nōmentānus?
> hoc mihi reddit ager: tē, Line, nōn videō!

hī omnēs, tamen, ob epigrammata Martiālia nunc cīvēs nōtissimī sunt. fortasse illī dē eō, sīcut ille dē eīs, dīcere possunt: 25

> difficilis facilis, iūcundus acerbus es īdem;
> nōn tēcum possum vīvere nec sine tē.

scrīptor *writer*
composuit: compōnere *compose*
ingenium: ingenium *talent*
epigramma: epigramma *epigram*
assentīre *agree*
aut...aut *either...or*
vetulās: vetulus *old*
turpēs: turpis *ugly, nasty*
vetulīs foediōrēs *more repulsive than old people*
convīvia: convīvium *party, banquet*
porticūs: porticus *colonnade*
formōsa: formōsus *beautiful*
tinctīs: tingere *color, dye*
capillīs: capillus *hair*

corvus *crow*
cȳcnus *swan*
fallis: fallere *trick, deceive*
Prōserpina *Proserpina (wife of Pluto in the Underworld)*
cānum: cānus *white, gray*
persōnam: persōna *mask (of an actor)*
dētrahet: dētrahere *pull down*
Nōmentānus *at Nomentum (a town 14 miles north-east of Rome)*
ob *because of*
iūcundus *sweet, pleasant*
acerbus *sour, bitter*
īdem *at the same time*

Questions

1 What did the writer, Pliny, do after Martial's death and why?
2 According to the last line of the first poem, what kind of impression does Fabulla want to make on people?
3 According to the rest of the poem, how does she try to do this?
4 According to the first line of the second poem, how does Laetinus try to fool his friends?
5 How does the second line reinforce that point?
6 When Martial suggests in the last line that "Proserpina will pull down the mask from your head," to what event is he probably referring?
7 How does Linus attempt to belittle Martial's villa?
8 According to Martial's poem on this subject, what is one good thing he gets from living at his villa?
9 What has Martial accomplished for the subjects of these three poems by featuring them in his epigrams?
10 Explain how the last poem (**difficilis facilis...**) might summarize their feelings about him and his feelings about them.

lībertus ūtilissimus

I

Translate the following story.

Epaphrodītus per ātrium aulae festīnat. nam ab Imperātōre mediā nocte arcessītus, nescit cūr Domitiānus sibi dīcere velit. crēdit tamen Imperātōrem uxōrem revocāre cōnstituisse. cubiculum intrat ut cum Domitiānō loquātur:

Domitiānus: mī Epaphrodīte, dormīre nōn possum, quod Domitia
            abest. putō eam revocārī dēbēre.   5
Epaphrodītus: sed, domine, sī eam tam celeriter revocāveris, omnēs
            Rōmānī tē rīdēbunt. nam scīs tē Paride, occīsō Domitiāque
            relēgātā, magnō ē perīculō servātum esse. nunc autem
            alius pantomīmus Paridī simillimus effēcit ut tū dē
            Domitiā cōgitēs. ego imperābō ut ille necētur.   10

pantomīmus *(pantomime) actor*

II

Read the rest of the story and answer the questions at the end.

hōc pantomīmō occīsō, Imperātor paulīsper dē Domitiā tacet. quondam eī obviam it Aelius Lamia, marītus prīmus Domitiae. nam Domitia, ut ā Domitiānō in mātrimōnium dūcerētur, Aelium repudiāvit. Imperātor, Aelium cōnspicātus, rogat:

Domitiānus: tūne, postquam Domitia tē repudiāvit, aliquam alteram in   5
            mātrimōnium dūxistī?
Aelius: cūr rogās, domine? fortasse tū aliam uxōrem quaeris?

Domitiānus, īrā perculsus, Epaphrodītō imperat ut Aelius removeātur. quō factō,
Imperātor per paucōs diēs contentus manet. tum lībertum iterum arcessit:

Domitiānus: (*libellum tenēns*) quis hunc libellum scrīpsit?   10
Epaphrodītus: cūr rogās, domine?
Domitiānus: hīc! hīc lege! auctor nārrat Paridem, prīncipem Trōiānum,
                 uxōrem Oenōnēn repudiāvisse. nōnne putās auctōrem rē
                 vērā dē mē Domitiāque loquī? praetereā Paris erat nōmen
                 pantomīmī quem Domitia amābat. ego certē crēdō hunc   15
                 auctōrem mē dērīdēre.
Epaphrodītus: Helvidius Priscus hunc libellum scrīpsit. gēns eius
                 perīculōsa est. imperābō ut ille necētur.
Domitiānus: (*Epaphrodītō ēgressō*) lībertus ūtilissimus es, Epaphrodīte.
                 tū etiam Imperātōrem Nerōnem adiūvistī, cum eī   20
                 pugiōnem offerrēs quō sē necāret. sed quondam imperābō
                 ut tū necēris, Epaphrodīte, quod nōlō tē mihi quoque
                 pugiōnem offerre.

in mātrimōnium dūcerētur: in   auctor *author*
  mātrimōnium dūcere *marry*   Trōiānum: Trōiānus *Trojan*
repudiāvit: repudiāre *divorce*   Oenōnēn: Oenōnē *Oenone (Paris' wife)*
perculsus: percellere *upset, strike*   perīculōsa: perīculōsus *dangerous*
libellum: libellus *booklet*   pugiōnem: pugiō *dagger*

Questions

1 Who is Aelius Lamia?
2 What does Domitian ask him when they meet?
3 What rather impertinent reply does Aelius give?
4 How does Domitian respond to this behavior?
5 What is the subject-matter of the book which Domitian shows
   Epaphroditus?
6 What does Domitian think is the real purpose of the book? Why does
   he think this?
7 What information does Epaphroditus supply about the author?
8 How does Epaphroditus propose handling the situation?
9 What example of Epaphroditus' usefulness does Domitian recall after
   his freedman has left?
10 What prediction does Domitian make about Epaphroditus' future?
11 Why does he feel this action will be necessary?

dē fēlīcitāte Agricolae

The following paragraphs are adapted from the biography of Agricola, written by his son-in-law, Tacitus.

I

Read through this eulogy and answer the questions at the end.

nātus erat Agricola Gāiō Caesare tertium cōnsule, Īdibus Iūniīs; mortuus est quārtō et quīnquāgēsimō annō, decimam Kalendās Septembris, Collegā Priscīnōque cōnsulibus. fortasse posterī scīre velint habitum eius fuisse decentiōrem quam sublīmiōrem; nihil impetūs in vultū vīsum esse; grātiam ōris superfuisse. facile erat crēdere eum bonum virum esse;   5
iūcundum erat eum virum magnum. ipse, quamquam mediō in spatiō integrae aetātis nōbīs ēreptus est, tamen ob glōriam bene meritam vītam "longissimam" perēgit. cōnsulārī atque triumphālibus ōrnāmentīs praeditus, satis pecūniae nactus, fīliā atque uxōre adhūc vīventibus, fēlīx mortuus est, antequam mala Imperātōris crūdēlissimī eī nocērent.   10

fēlīcitāte: fēlīcitās *good luck*
tertium *for the third time*
Īdibus Iūniīs *on June 13*
quīnquāgēsimō: quīnquāgēsimus *fiftieth*
decimam Kalendās Septembris *on August 23*
posterī *descendants, posterity*
habitum: habitus *personal appearance*
decentiōrem: decēns *handsome*
sublīmiōrem: sublīmis *imposing*
nihil impetūs: nihil impetūs *nothing violent*
grātiam ōris: grātia ōris *kindliness of expression*
iūcundum: iūcundus *pleasant, agreeable*
spatiō: spatium *space, period, point of time*
integrae aetātis: integer aetās *prime of life*
ob *because of*
perēgit: peragere *live*
cōnsulārī: cōnsulāris *of an ex-consul, consular*
triumphālibus: triumphālis *of a triumph*
   (*celebratory procession following military success*)
praeditus *endowed with, provided with*
nactus: nancīscī *obtain*
antequam *before*

Questions

1 How does Tacitus refer to the years of Agricola's birth and death?
2 How old was Agricola when he died?
3 Summarize Tacitus' description of Agricola's personal appearance.
4 What reason does he give for including these details?
5 What judgment would it be easy to make about Agricola?
6 What other opinion of Agricola would it be pleasant to believe?
7 In what respect could you say that Agricola lived a long life?
8 In the last sentence, Tacitus suggests four quite different reasons for feeling that Agricola died **fēlīx**. What are those four reasons?

II

Translate the following continuation of the eulogy, which explains Agricola's **fēlīcitās** *by criticizing Domitian's actions in the years since Agricola died.*

nōs, nōn Agricola, vidēmus cūriam obsessam et senātum mīlitibus
circumdatum esse; dē tot cōnsulārum caede, tot nōbilissimārum
fēminārum exsiliō cognōscimus. scīmus sententiās Catullī Messālīnī, cum
Agricola ab Imperātōre honōrārētur, in cūriam nōndum pervēnisse;
Helvidium in carcerem nōndum iactum esse; Flāvium Clēmentem,   5
Acīlium Glabriōnem nōndum occīsōs esse.

　　Nerō, cum prīnceps esset, subtrāxit oculōs iussitque scelera, nōn
spectāvit. Domitiānus autem nōn sōlum spectat sed adest ut nōtet num
quī amīcī pallidō vultū significent sē victimae favēre, Imperātōrem
dēspicere.   10

cūriam: cūria *senate-house*	**honōrārētur: honōrāre** *honor*
obsessam: obsidēre *besiege*	**subtrāxit: subtrahere** *turn away, avert*
circumdatum: circumdare *surround*	**nōtet: nōtāre** *note, mark down*
cōnsulārum: cōnsulāris *ex-consul,*	**num quī** *whether any, if any*
man of consular rank	**significent: significāre** *indicate, signify*
caede: caedēs *murder, killing*	**dēspicere** *despise*
exsiliō: exsilium *exile*	

epistula perīculōsa

I

Translate the following letter.

C. Helvidius Lupus salūtem dīcit Acīliō Glabriōnī amīcō.

pro certō habeō tē, verbīs meīs lēctīs, lacrimātūrum esse. nam tibi
nūntiō fīlium meum mortuum esse. fortasse meministī eum ē vīllā nostrā
discessisse et puellam aliquam in urbe vīsitāvisse. nescio cūr puellam
adamāverit quae sit adfīnis Imperātōris. nescio cūr oblītus sit gentem   5
nostram Imperātōrī odiō esse. sed scio mentem corde saepe regī.

perīculōsa: perīculōsus *dangerous*	**adamāverit: adamāre** *fall in love with*
meministī *you remember*	**adfīnis** *relative*
aliquam: aliquī *some*	**corde: cor** *heart*

II

Read the rest of the letter and answer the questions at the end.

Pōlla, puella quam fīlius meus amāvit, est fīlia T. Flāviī Clēmentis.
Domitiānus, caudex quī putat adfīnēs (sīcut cēterōs Rōmānōs) servōs
esse, Clēmentī imperāvit ut Pōlla Sparsō nūberet. cōgitā stultitiam
hominis! ille bene scit Pōllam quattuordecim annōs nātam esse, Sparsum
quīnquāgintā. tamen, quod dīcit sē fīliōs Clēmentis ascītūrum esse, crēdit   5
sē fīliam quoque possidēre.

filius meus intellegere nōn poterat cūr Pōlla sibi nūbere prōhibita
esset. itaque diē quō illa Sparsō nūptūra esset, domum Sparsī prōfectus,
eum prō iānuā stantem pugiōne petīvit. deinde ā servīs superātus, ad
Imperātōrem ductus est, quī eum occīdī iussit.   10

pater huius Imperātōris ōlim patrem meum ad mortem mīsit; nunc
fīlius eius meum fīlium necāvit. ego ipse istam bēstiam occīdere volō.
attonitusne es? ego, quī tē saepe monuī nē Imperātōrem offendās, quī tibi
saepe scrīpsī ut caveās, nunc Domitiānum apertē vituperō atque accūsō?
nihil cūrō! sīcut fīlius Pōllam amāvit, ego fīlium amāvī. sīcut pater   15
fīliusque meus mortem nōn timēbant, ego quoque perīre audeō. nōlī
monēre ut caveam! caveat Imperātor! valē!

caudex *blockhead, idiot*	**bēstiam: bēstia** *wild animal, beast*
stultitiam: stultitia *stupidity*	**apertē** *openly*
quattuordecim *fourteen*	**caveat Imperātor** *if* **caveat ēmptor**
ascītūrum esse: ascīscere *adopt*	*means "Let the buyer beware," you can*
possidēre *own, possess*	*probably see what Helvidius' comment*
pugiōne: pugio *dagger*	*here means*

Questions

1 What comment does Helvidius make about Domitian's attitude towards family members?
2 Why does he feel that the emperor is also stupid?
3 What reasoning does he feel lies behind Domitian's actions in determining Polla's husband?
4 According to the first sentence of the second paragraph, what explanation does Helvidius make for his son's subsequent actions?
5 What is one detail from the story we read in Stage 38 that Helvidius repeats in his letter?
6 What is one detail he gives which is not in that story?
7 What wish does Helvidius express in the last paragraph?
8 Why does he feel that Glabrio will be surprised by the opinions he expresses in the letter?
9 What two explanations/justifications does Helvidius offer for his behavior?
10 What anticipated warning from Glabrio does he reject?
11 Instead, what warning does he himself issue?

I

Translate the following story.

Pōlla, fīlia Titī Flāviī Clēmentis, patrī dē coniuge Sparsō queritur. Clēmēns, quod scit Pōllam Sparsō invītam nūpsisse, dē hāc rē loquī nōn vult. illa tamen patrem ōrat ut verba sua audiat:

Pōlla: nescio, pater, cūr ego istī senī nūbere coācta sim. nescio cūr tū
              vītam mihi miserrimam reddiderīs. scio tantum hunc   *5*
              prōditōrem in vīllā nostrā per noctem numquam manēre; eum
              cum aliīs fēminīs saepe vīsum esse; mē propter hās causās ab
              amīcīs meīs dērīdērī. crēdō equidem mē illum...aut mē
              ipsam...necātūram esse, nisi hanc perfidiam dēsierit.

Clēmēns: quamquam valdē perturbāris, mea Pōlla, inūtile est querī. ego   *10*
              ipse multa odiōsa facere cōgor, nē Imperātor Domitiānus
              familiam meam pūniat. nōnne cōnsentīs etiam vītam
              miserrimam meliōrem esse quam vītam nūllam?

contentiō *argument*	**equidem** *indeed*
reddiderīs: reddere *make, render*	**dēsierit: dēsinere** *stop, cease*
prōditōrem: prōditor *traitor*	**odiōsa: odiōsus** *hateful*
propter *because of*	

II

Read the rest of the story and answer the questions at the end.

Pōlla: pater, ignāvissimus es! mortem quam vītam miserrimam mālō.
num oblītus es Helvidium, quem valdē amāvī, periisse, ā
mīlitibus praetōriānīs occīsum? tē intellegere oportet mē
quoque mortem nōn timēre.

Clēmēns: cūr istum iuvenem commemorās? Helvidius sānē stultissimus,   *5*
nōn fortissimus, fuit, sīcut avus eius, quī, quamquam senātor
nōtissimus erat, Imperātōrem Vespasiānum vituperāre ausus,
poenam morte suō dedit; et sīcut patruus, quī, quod fābulās in
theātrō ēdit, quae familiam Imperātōris dērīdēre videntur,
Domitiānum maximē offendit. intellegere nōn possum cūr tū   *10*
hanc gentem laudēs.

Pōlla: gentem Helvidiī laudō, quod illī virī fortiter perīre sciunt. sine
dubiō tū, sīcut frāter tuus, ignōminiōsē perībis. quī, cōnsul
ēlēctus, odiō Domitiānō factus est, quod praecō verbō
"Imperātōre" prō "cōnsule" forte ūsus est. tālī Imperātōrī   *15*
assentārī nōn modum ignāvum sed etiam inūtile est.

Clēmēns: et cum tālī Imperātōre dissentīre quoque inūtile est.
Domitiānus ipse marītum tuum ēlēgit. sī tū Sparsum, aut tē
ipsam, occīderis, patrem tuum et mātrem ob īram Imperātōris
quoque interficiēs. tibi ēligendum est...   *20*

praetōriānīs: praetōriānus *praetorian*	**praecō** *herald, announcer*
avus *grandfather*	**prō** *instead of*
ausus *having dared*	**ūsus est: ūtī** *use (+ ablative)*
patruus *uncle*	**assentārī** *always agree with, flatter*
videntur: vidērī *seem*	**ob** *because of*
ignōminiōsē *ignominiously, disgracefully*	

Questions

1 How does Polla answer her father's question from Part I?
2 Why does she feel her father should understand this?
3 In response, what characteristic does Clemens attach to the behavior
of Helvidius and his family?
4 In your own words, outline <u>either</u> of the two examples he provides of
that characteristic.
5 What characteristic does Polla attach to the behavior of her own father
and his family, in comparison with Helvidius' family?
6 Explain how she uses the death of her father's brother to make her
point.
7 What ominous prediction does Clemens make to his daughter in a last
effort to "talk sense" into her?

rhētor dēceptus

I

Translate the following story.

Titus Pūbliusque, fīliī Clēmentis, libellum poētae Ovidiī legunt, ad versūs rhētorī Quīntiliānō postrīdiē recitandōs. Titus, quod scit rhētorem rogātūrum esse ut prīmus recitet, frātrī queritur:

Titus: nōnne putās, mī Pūblī, hunc Quīntiliānum esse hominem
           stultissimum? nam tū, quamquam verēris nē tibi prīmō   5
           recitandum sit, semper post mē rogēris.
Pūblius: crēdō rhētorem hoc semper fēcisse, quod tū, māior nātū, melius
           recitās. animadvertō quoque tē, ōrātiōnibus perfectīs, saepius
           quam mē laudārī.
Titus: cōnsilium ergō habeō! crās rogābimur ut hōs versūs recitēmus.   10
           Quīntiliānus nōn rogābit num rem tōtam didicerīmus. sī ego
           prīmam carminis partem parāverō, tū secundam, rhētor
           numquam intelleget sē falsum esse.
Pūblius: mihi placet!

libellum: libellus *booklet*   **māior nātū** *being older*
versūs: versus *verse, line (of poetry)*

II

Read the rest of the story and answer the questions at the end.

postrīdiē puerī, ad aulam regressī, ā Quīntiliānō salutantur.

Quīntiliānus: salvēte, Tite Pūblīque! heri versūs quōsdam poētae Ovidiī
discere conābāminī. spērō vōs hoc carmen hodiē recitāre
posse. sed prīmum velim hanc fābulam verbīs vestrīs atque
ōrātiōne solūtā audīre. Tite, incipe!   5

Titus: Pȳramus, iuvenum pulcherrimus, et Thisbē, omnibus
puellīs praelāta, contiguās tenuērunt domōs. tempore crēvit
amor...sed nūptiās vetuērunt patrēs! amantēs tamen,
quamquam eīs inter sē vīsitāre nōn licēbat, labrīs in rīmam
parietis tenuem pōnendīs, susurrāre ōsculaque dare   10
solēbant. tandem, amōre audāciāque adductī, cōnstituērunt
ut nocte silentī fallere custōdēs foribusque excēdere
temptārent et convenīrent extrā urbem sub umbrā arboris
nōtissimae:

> arbor ibī niveīs ūberrima pōmīs   15
> ardua mōrus erat, gelidō contermina fontī.

eā nocte Thisbē, quam audācem faciēbat amor, prīma ad
arborem pervēnit. ecce! vēnit leaena, caede recentī boum
oblita, aquae fontis bibendae causā.

> quam procul ad lūnae radiōs Babylōnia Thisbē   20
> vīdit, et obscūrum trepidō pede fūgit in antrum
> dumque fugit, tergō vēlāmina lāpsa relīquit.

Pȳramus, sērius domō ēgressus, ad arborem vēnit. cum
vestem sanguine tinctam repperisset (quod leaena
vēlāmina ōre cruentātō laniāverat), timēbat nē Thisbē   25
mortua esset.

> "ūna duōs," inquit, "nox perdet amantēs!"

haec locūtus, ōsculīsque vestī datīs, sē gladiō necāvit.

> arboreī fētūs adspergine caedis in ātram
> vertuntur faciem, madefactaque sanguine rādīx   30
> purpureō tingit pendentia mōra colōre.

Titus loquī dēsinit, quod crēdit rhētorem Pūblium rogātūrum esse ut cēterōs
versūs nārret. Quīntiliānus tamen Titō signum dat ut ōrātiōnem renovet. ille,
quod versūs cēterōs frātrī mandāvit, nescit quid dīcat. celeriter tamen cōnsilium
capit, et Quīntiliānō explicat: 35

Titus: domine, hanc fābulam renovāre nōn possum. quotiēns dē
                Pȳramō Thisbēque nārrō, dē Pōllā, sorōre nostrā, et
                Helvidiō, amātō eius, putō. rem difficilem...

Quīntiliānus, quī dē amōre Pōllae et morte Helvidiī intellegit, hīs verbīs fallitur.
posteā tamen Titus Pūbliusque omnēs versūs discunt!   40

prīmum *first*	**boum** (= **bovum**): **bovēs** *cattle*
ōrātiōne solūtā *in prose speech*	**oblita: oblinere** *smear*
praelāta: praelātus *surpassing*	**radiōs: radius** *ray*
contiguās: contiguus *attached, adjoining*	**Babylōnia: Babylōnius** *Babylonian*
crēvit: crēscere *grow, increase*	**obscūrum: obscūrus** *dark*
nūptiās: nūptiae *marriage*	**trepidō: trepidus** *trembling*
vetuērunt: vetāre *forbid*	**antrum: antrum** *cave*
eīs licēbat: mihi licet *I am permitted,*	**tergō: tergum** *back*
I may	**vēlāmina: vēlāmen** *veil, covering*
labrīs: labrum *lip*	**lāpsa: lābī** *slip, fall*
rīmam: rīma *crack*	**sērius** *later*
parietis: pariēs *house wall, (common) wall*	**tinctam: tingere** *stain*
tenuem: tenuis *thin*	**repperisset: reperīre** *find*
susurrāre *whisper*	**ōre: ōs** *mouth*
adductī: addūcere *lead on, influence*	**cruentātō: cruentātus** *bloody*
silentī: silēns *silent*	**laniāverat: laniāre** *tear to pieces*
foribus *out, out of doors*	**arboreī: arboreus** *of the tree*
niveīs: niveus *snow-white*	**fētūs: fētus** *fruit*
ūberrima: ūber *fertile, rich, abundant*	**adspergine: adspergō** *spray*
pōmīs: pōmum *fruit*	**ātram: āter** *dark, black*
ardua: arduus *tall*	**faciem: faciēs** *appearance, face*
mōrus *mulberry tree*	**madefacta: madefactus** *wet*
gelidō: gelidus *cold, icy*	**rādīx** *root, base*
contermina: conterminus *close to*	**purpureō: purpureus** *dark red*
leaena *lioness*	**pendentia: pendēre** *hang down*
caede: caedēs *slaughter, killing*	**mōra: mōrum** *mulberry*
recentī: recēns *recent*	**renovet: renovāre** *renew, resume*

Questions

1 What does Quintilian want the boys to do first?
2 How does the poet Ovid describe Pyramus and Thisbe?
3 Where did they live?
4 What problem did they encounter in their love affair?
5 How did they manage to communicate with one another?
6 What bold plan did they eventually try to carry out?
7 What are two details about their meeting place that Ovid gives in the first poetic excerpt?
8 What frightening experience did Thisbe have?
9 What action did she take?
10 What mistaken impression did Pyramus have when he arrived?
11 Why did he come to this conclusion?
12 What action did he take?
13 In his *Metamorphoses* (the poem from which this story is taken), Ovid often likes to give a poetic legend for the origin of certain changes in nature. In the first and last poetry excerpts quoted by Titus, Ovid explains how the color of the mulberry fruit changed and why. In your own words, summarize the explanation he provides, giving the change and the reason.
14 What clever explanation does Titus think of for not being able to continue the story?
15 What lesson do the boys learn from their experience?

40.1   patrōnus miserrimus

I

Translate the following story.

Gāius Salvius Līberālis, cum intellēxisset sē in
exilium mittī, fīlium paucōsque amīcōs quī eum
adiūverant ad grātiās eīs agendās arcessīvit. fīliō
adstante, affirmāvit sē eīs semper fāvisse neque
favōris eōrum umquam oblītūrum esse.

5

  "sī verēminī," inquit, "nē prīnceps vōs quoque
pūniat, hortor ut mē in exilium sequāminī."

  Haterius, cliēns Salviī, celeriter prōcēdendō, sē
cum patrōnō iūnxit.

adstante: adstāre *stand by, stand near*

II

Read the rest of the story and answer the questions at the end.

postrīdiē Haterius, vīllam Salviī ingressus, patrōnum librum intentē
spectantem invēnit. ille, clientem cōnspicātus, trīstis nūntiāvit sē verba
poētae Ovidiī legere.

"Ovidius," inquit, "ab imperātōre suō in exilium quoque damnātus,
hōs versūs familiae amīcīsque valedīcendī causā scrīpsit: 5

> alloquor extrēmum <u>maestōs</u> abitūrus <u>amīcōs</u>,
>   quī modo dē multīs ūnus et alter erat.
> <u>uxor</u> <u>amāns</u> flentem <u>flēns</u> ācrius <u>ipsa</u> tenēbat,
>   <u>imbre</u> per *indignās* usque <u>cadente</u> *genās*.
> <u>nāta</u> procul *Libycīs* aberat <u>dīversa</u> sub *ōrīs*   10
>   nec poterat <u>fātī</u> certior esse <u>meī</u>."

Salvius, hīs verbīs recitātīs, librum in lectum dēposuit atque lacrimīs
sē dedit.

versūs: versus *verse, line (of poetry)*	**indignās: indignus** *guiltless*
alloquor: alloquī *speak to, address*	**usque** *continually*
extrēmum *for the last time*	**genās: gena** *cheek*
maestōs: maestus *sad*	**nāta** *daughter*
modo *just now, recently*	**Libycīs: Libycus** *Libyan, African*
dē multīs *reduced from many*	**dīversa: dīversus** *remote, distant, far off*
ūnus et alter *one or two*	**ōrīs: ōra** *shore, land*
flentem: flēre *weep*	**fātī: fātum** *fate, fortune*
ācrius *more bitterly*	**certior esse** *be informed (of)*
imbre: imber *rain, showers, tears*	

Notes to assist with the poem

- Some noun-and-adjective phrases, in which an adjective is separated by one
  word or more from the noun which it describes, have been underlined. Where
  there is more than one such phrase in a line, the second phrase has been put in
  italics.
- **abitūrus** (line 1 of the poem) describes the subject of **alloquor**.
- **flentem** (line 3 of the poem) describes **mē** (understood), the writer of the poem.

Questions

1 What was Salvius doing when Haterius arrived?
2 Before reading Ovid's poem aloud, what did Salvius say its purpose was?
3 In the first two lines of the poem, find one similarity to Salvius' present situation.
4 Explain how Salvius' situation and the situation of Ovid in lines 3 and 4 of the poem are different, to Salvius' disadvantage. (You will need to remember what happened in Stage 40 to answer this.)
5 Explain how Salvius' situation and the situation of Ovid in lines 5 and 6 of the poem are different, to Salvius' advantage.
6 What was Salvius' reaction when he finished his recitation?

40.2   Haterius reputat

I

Translate the following story.

Quīntus Haterius Latrōniānus, postquam Salviō pollicitus est sē
patrōnum in exilium comitātūrum esse, domum ad hoc uxōrī
nūntiandum festīnāvit. quō cōnsiliō audītō, Vitellia exīstimāvit marītum
īnsāniā affectum esse. crēdere nōn poterat eum tāle iter cōgitāre.
   "intellegisne," inquit, "tē patrōnō sequendō uxōrem familiamque 5
prōdidisse? praetereā timeō nē Imperātor, tē ēgressō, nōs omnēs pūniat."

reputat: reputāre *reconsider*   **īnsāniā: īnsānia** *insanity, madness*

II

Read the rest of the story and answer the questions which follow.

Vitellia, haec verba locūta, ē vīllā contendit et domum patris, sorōris
Rūfillae quaerendae causā, petīvit. Haterius, in vīllā sōlus relictus, librum
legere coepit, in quō versūs poētae Ovidiī invēnit:

> at cum trīstis hiēms <u>squālentia</u> prōtulit <u>ōra</u>
> terraque *marmoreō* est <u>candida</u> facta *gelū*,   5
> saepe sonant <u>mōtī</u> glaciē pendente <u>capillī</u>,
> et nitet <u>inductō</u> candida barba <u>gelū</u>,
> <u>nūda</u>que cōnsistunt, formam <u>servantia</u> testae
> <u>vīna</u>, nec hausta merī sed data frūsta bibunt.
> quid loquar ut <u>vinctī</u> concrēscant frīgore <u>rīvī</u>   10
> dēque lacū <u>fragilēs</u> effodiantur <u>aquae</u>?

Haterius, dum haec verba īnspicit, perterritus fīēbat. nam poēta
Ovidius dē exiliō suō nārrābat. Haterius verērī coepit nē ad terram
similem cum Salviō exīret. librō in vīllā relictō, domum patris Vitelliae
petīvit uxōris quaerendae causā.   15

versūs: versus *verse, line (of poetry)*	**formam: forma** *form*
squālentia: squālēns *rough, stiff*	**testae: testa** *jug, pot*
prōtulit: prōferre *bring forth, reveal*	**hausta merī** *draughts (swallows) of wine*
ōra: ōs *face, appearance*	**frūsta: frūstum** *bit, piece, morsel*
marmoreō: marmoreus *like marble*	**quid** *why*
candida: candidus *white, bright*	**ut** *how*
gelū: gelus *frost, icy cold(ness)*	**vinctī: vincīre** *bind, fetter, enchain*
sonant: sonāre *resound, make a noise*	**concrēscant: concrēscere** *become stiff, harden*
glaciē: glaciēs *ice, hardness*	
pendente: pendēre *hang down*	**frīgore: frīgus** *cold(ness)*
nitet: nitēre *shine, glitter*	**rīvī: rīvus** *stream*
inductō: indūcere *spread over, put on*	**dē** *from*
barba *beard*	**lacū: lacus** *lake*
nūda: nūdus *bare*	**fragilēs: fragilis** *crackling, fragile*
cōnsistunt: cōnsistere *stop, freeze*	**effodiantur: effodere** *dig out*

Notes to assist with the poem

- Some noun-and-adjective phrases, in which an adjective is separated by one
  word or more from the noun which it describes, have been underlined. Where
  there is more than one such phrase in a line, the second phrase has been put in
  italics.
- The verb in line 2 of the poem is **facta est** (from **fierī**).
- Supply "they" (= "people") as the subject of **bibunt** in line 6 of the poem.

Questions

1 What did Vitellia do after her comments at the end of Part I of the story?
2 For what purpose did she take this action?
3 What did Haterius do?
4 Ovid's poem is full of winter details that are almost ridiculous:
  a **capillī sonant** (line 3 of the poem). Explain why this happens.
  b **barba nitet** (line 4 of the poem). Explain why this happens.
  c What happens to the wine in line 5 of the poem?
  d As a result, what do people drink, instead of **hausta merī**?
  e In the last line of his poem, Ovid describes an activity that would have appeared strange to his Roman readers, but which is not uncommon in areas where fresh-water lakes freeze solid in the winter. What is that activity?
5 After reading this poem about Ovid's exile, what worry did Haterius have?
6 What did he do, as a result?

74

Answer Key

Teachers may use their discretion in accepting valid alternatives.

22.1 Modestus Finds a Curse Tablet

After Modestus pulled himself out of the spring, he stood there, cursing Vilbia and Bulbus. Suddenly he heard someone entering the baths. The terrified soldier hid behind a column, from where he caught sight of a Roman senator.

The senator, having entered the baths, silently approached the spring, carrying a curse tablet. Then after he hurled the tablet into the spring, he left quickly.

Because Modestus was now soaked through, he jumped into the spring and found the tablet which had been thrown down by the senator. He read these words: Cogidubnus must die.

22.2 Modestus the Liar

Strythio was walking through the streets of the town of Aquae Sulis, searching for his friend, Modestus. Suddenly he caught sight of the soldier leaving the baths. Modestus, (because he was) soaked through, was moving slowly.

"Modestus!" shouted Strythio. "Why are you so wet? Who did this?"

Modestus showed Strythio a curse tablet which he had found in the spring.

"That Bulbus," he said, "tricked me. Today he came to the baths, carrying this curse tablet. After he entered the baths, he threw the tablet down into the spring. The words written on the tablet pleased the goddess Sulis. The goddess dragged me into the spring."

22.3 Very Brave Soldiers

I

Modestus, a very wretched soldier, was sitting in Terentius's tavern. (He was now afraid to visit Latro's tavern!) Draining a goblet of wine, he thought this to himself:

"Because I was tricked by Bulbus, I fell into the sacred spring. I almost died, because this water was very hot. When Vilbia entered the baths, she heard my shouts and cursed me a lot. Now all my friends make fun of me."

Suddenly Strythio entered the tavern, looking for Modestus. Because Modestus caught sight of Strythio first, he shouted:

"Strythio, come here! I want you to help me. Don't say no! You are a very clever man. How can I punish that Bulbus?"

"O Modestus," replied his friend, "you have drunk too much wine. A drunk soldier cannot defeat any enemies. However, listen to me! I have an excellent plan, sent by the goddess Sulis."

II

Modestus, warned by Strythio, put his goblet on the table and remained silent, listening to his friend.

Strythio said, "We must make a curse. We can throw this curse, written on a tablet, into the sacred spring. Then, when we have prayed to the goddess, we can wait for revenge. That Bulbus punished you this way; you can punish him this way!"

And so the next day, the two friends hurried to the baths. However, they stopped in the doorway of the spring. For someone, standing near the spring, was throwing a charm into the water.

"Isn't that Salvius, a Roman senator?" whispered Modestus. "Why would a senator want to come to this spring?"

Suddenly Salvius caught sight of the soldiers and ordered them to come nearer to the spring. Looking intently at their faces, he asked,

"Why have you come to the sacred spring? What do you want? Answer quickly!"

Modestus, a very brave soldier, fell unconscious to the floor. Strythio, however, began:

"My friend, we want to throw a curse tablet down into the water. For Bulbus, a deceitful man, tricked my friend and stole his girl. Now..."

"Blockhead!" shouted Salvius. "The Britons, who are barbarian people, believe in the goddess Sulis, but it is not proper for Romans to carry out this nonsense."

Then he hurried quickly from the baths.

Strythio, who had seen Salvius throwing down the charm, said nothing. But he stepped forward to the spring and looked for this charm in the water. When he finally got hold of the charm, he read in astonishment: Death to King Cogidubnus.

Strythio fell unconscious next to Modestus!

Answers to Comprehension Questions

1   He and Modestus would make a curse tablet against Bulbus, throw it in the sacred spring, pray to the goddess and wait for revenge.
2   It appeared to have worked for Bulbus, according to Modestus.
3   They caught sight of someone throwing a charm into the spring.
4   The man was Salvius, a Roman senator, and Modestus could not understand why such a man would want to come to the spring.

5   Modestus fainted (fell unconscious to the floor).
6   He suggested that it was sacred only to barbarians like the Britons, who believed in the goddess Sulis. Such beliefs were nonsense.
7   Strythio had seen Salvius throwing the charm in the spring. Why would someone who felt such actions were nonsense do such a thing?
8   He read: Death to King Cogidubnus.

23.1   Modestus the Priest

I

Strythio was sitting in Latro's tavern in the town of Aquae Sulis. Suddenly Modestus rushed through the doorway, shouting,

"Help me, Strythio! I have to hide very quickly."

"What is it, Modestus?" replied his friend. "I have never seen you so frightened."

"A messenger, whom the commander has sent, is here. He is carrying instructions, which order me to return to the camp. Strythio, you are a very clever man. I don't want to go back to the fighting. I would like to live longer. Where can I hide?"

When Modestus had said this, he was almost in tears. Bulbus and Gutta, who were playing dice near Strythio's table, laughed strongly. However, Strythio said nothing, because he was trying to devise a plan. Then, getting up, he said to Modestus,

"Come with me to the temple of Sulis Minerva. Today the goddess favors you. Today you become a priest."

II

Memor, the manager of the baths, with two priests, was sacrificing a victim in the temple. When Salvius burst into the shrine, he ordered Memor to dismiss the priests.

"But, my dear Salvius," said Memor, "we have to sacrifice this rooster to the goddess Minerva. Surely you wouldn't want us to offend the goddess?"

"I couldn't care less about the goddess!" replied Salvius. "We have to talk alone. Dismiss the priests at once!"

The astonished priests left the temple. Then, after Salvius looked around cautiously, he said angrily to Memor,

"You have acted very stupidly, my dear manager. You have almost managed (procured) death for all of us. Why did you choose Cephalus? You ought to have carried out a task of this sort yourself."

"But Cephalus wanted to carry out this task himself," replied Memor. "Cephalus himself wanted me to give the poison to him. Cephalus was wrong; I wasn't wrong. Cephalus was a man of very little courage."

"You are a man of very little courage," shouted Salvius. "Why did you begin to say 'Salvius...' to Cogidubnus, after the king removed you from the management of the baths? I would like to hear the rest of the words. What were you going to say?"

"My dear Salvius..."

"Quiet!" whispered Salvius. "I see something behind that column."

Salvius ran to the column. There he found Modestus trembling.

"Who is this?" he asked. "What kind of priest is he?"

"He is no priest," replied Memor. "He is Modestus, a sick soldier...and a very cowardly soldier!"

"What did you hear?" demanded Salvius. "What were we saying?"

"Cephalus...Cephalus..." But Modestus could not say anything more.

"What do you know about Cephalus?" asked Salvius.

"Memor killed Cephalus," shouted Modestus. "Memor gave him poison. Memor tried to tell Cogidubnus, 'Salvius did this...'"

"You are making a big mistake," Memor began to say, but Salvius said, "You are speaking the truth. Memor did this, but Cephalus was a man of evil character. Memor had to kill him. And you must say nothing about this matter. Now I have to hurry to Cogidubnus' palace and you have to return to the camp at Deva. Away!"

Modestus ran out of the temple as quickly as he could. Salvius left smiling. Memor stood in the temple, the height of misery.

Answers to Comprehension Questions

1   He and two priests were making a sacrifice.
2   He told Memor to dismiss the priests.
3   He said they would offend the goddess if they interrupted the sacrifice.
4   He is insensitive / has no respect for the gods.
5   Salvius wanted to talk about Memor's handling of the attempted assassination of Cogidubnus.
6   He felt Memor should have done the job himself.
7   He blamed Cephalus because Cephalus had insisted Memor turn things over to him, and then displayed a lack of courage.
8   He wanted to know what Memor was going to say to Cogidubnus when he blurted out "Salvius..." after Cogidubnus dismissed Memor from his post as manager of the baths.
9   Salvius spotted something/someone behind a column.
10 It was Modestus, a sick and very cowardly soldier.

11 Modestus thought Memor had killed Cephalus by giving him poison and then had tried to blame Salvius.

12 He said that Modestus was right, but that the deed had to be done, because Cephalus was an evil man.

13 He now had a witness whose understanding of the "truth" would prevent Salvius' part in the assassination plot from being discovered.

Part II of 23.1 and Part II of 24.1 are mostly identical. Do not use both stories with the same group of students.

24.1 A Terrified Soldier

I

When Modestus had dragged himself slowly from the spring, he wanted to look for Strythio.

"We have to go back to Deva," he said, "because in this town, all the girls can now make fun of me. Since I was tricked by Bulbus, I am a very sad man!"

As he was saying these words to himself, he suddenly heard hostile voices. The terrified soldier prayed timidly to the goddess and very quickly hid behind a column, from where he caught sight of two men entering the baths. He recognized Memor and a Roman senator, who were angrily arguing. Modestus, soaked through and very wretched, lay on the floor (ground), listening to this argument.

II

"Blockhead!" shouted the senator. "Why did you choose Cephalus? You ought to have carried out a task of this sort yourself."

"But Cephalus wanted to carry out this task himself," replied Memor.

"Cephalus himself wanted me to give the poison to him. Cephalus was wrong; I wasn't wrong. Cephalus was a man of very little courage."

"You are a man of very little courage," shouted Salvius. "Why did you begin to say, 'Salvius...' to Cogidubnus, after the king removed you from the management of the baths? I would like to hear the rest of the words. What were you going to say?"

"My dear Salvius..."

Suddenly Modestus sneezed. Memor and Salvius looked around quickly. They proceeded to the column and found the trembling Modestus.

"Who is this?" Salvius asked. "What kind of priest is he?"

"He is no priest," replied Memor. "He is Modestus, a sick soldier...and a very cowardly soldier!"

"What did you hear?" demanded Salvius. "What were we saying?"

"Cephalus...Cephalus..." But Modestus could not say anything more.

"What do you know about Cephalus?" asked Salvius.

"Memor killed Cephalus," shouted Modestus. "Memor gave him poison. Memor tried to tell Cogidubnus, 'Salvius did this...'"

"You are making a big mistake," Memor began to say, but Salvius said, "You are speaking the truth. Memor did this, but Cephalus was a man of evil character. Memor had to kill him. And you must say nothing about this matter. Do you understand?"

"I understand well," replied Modestus, who understood nothing and wanted to understand nothing.

"Now," said Salvius, "I must hurry to Cogidubnus' palace and you must return to Deva. Away!"

Modestus ran out of the baths as quickly as he could. Salvius left smiling. Memor stood there, very wretched.

Answers to Comprehension Questions

1 They were arguing about Memor's handling of the attempted assassination of Cogidubnus.

2 He felt Memor should have done the job himself.

3 He said that Cephalus had insisted on doing the deed. He asked Memor to give him the poison.

4 He wanted to know what Memor was going to say to Cogidubnus when he blurted out "Salvius..." after Cogidubnus dismissed Memor from his post as manager of the baths.

5 Modestus thought Memor had killed Cephalus by giving him poison and then had tried to blame Salvius.

6 He said that Modestus was right, but that the deed had to be done, because Cephalus was an evil man.

7 He now had a witness whose understanding of the "truth" would prevent Salvius' part in the assassination plot from being discovered.

25.1 Strythio Offers Help

I

After Modestus and Strythio left the prison, they began to hurry toward the granaries. For Strythio, a very wise man, had explained how they could hide underneath a granary. However, when the two soldiers were proceeding silently through the camp, they suddenly caught sight of a man entering through the gate. Because Modestus understood who the man was, he whispered to Strythio:

"We have to get out of here! For this is Salvius, a man of great authority. When I fell into that spring in the town of Aquae Sulis, I found a curse tablet prepared by Salvius. He wants to kill King Cogidubnus."

II

When Modestus had said these words, he hid behind a near-by building, because he wanted to avoid Salvius. Strythio, however, a very courageous soldier, boldly approached Salvius.

"Greetings, my dear senator!" he said. "What are you looking for?"

"Greetings, friend!" replied Salvius. "I have just arrived in the camp. I must hurry to headquarters, because Agricola is waiting for me. You must take me to headquarters."

When Strythio heard this, he was very frightened.

"I don't want to go to headquarters with this senator," he thought to himself, "because if that centurion, Valerius, catches sight of me there, he can arrest me."

Since the soldier didn't know what he could say, he stood motionless. Salvius shouted more angrily:

"Why are you standing there, blockhead? Surely you can find the headquarters? I am a very powerful senator and I would like to speak with Agricola about very serious matters."

Suddenly, Strythio had a clever idea.

He said, "I am remaining here, sir, because I am waiting for my friend. We can take you to headquarters right away. My friend usually repairs buildings. He is now working behind that building. Hey! comrade!"

Modestus, very angry and very frightened, walked slowly towards Strythio and Salvius, silently cursing his friend. Meanwhile, Salvius, looking intently at the soldier, asked,

"Don't I recognize you? In the town of Aquae Sulis..."

"It was my brother...Hercules!" Modestus answered quickly. "My brother often visits the baths, because he is a very sick man."

Then, turning to Strythio, he whispered,

"Pest! Why did you call me out? What are you doing?"

Strythio, however, began to lead Salvius toward the granaries.

"Look! Headquarters!" he said.

Salvius, by now very angry, shouted:

"Are you blind? These buildings are the granaries, not headquarters!"

"Yes," replied Strythio. "These buildings are very similar to granaries. However, they are in fact the headquarters. Britons often attack this camp. They want to set fire to the headquarters. Therefore, we made the headquarters very much like the granaries and in this way tricked the Britons."

Then Strythio caught sight of the centurion Valerius coming out of the real headquarters. The soldier took Modestus with him and hurried behind the buildings, leaving Salvius in the middle of the road. Salvius, astonished, thought to himself,

"If soldiers like these are guarding the Roman Empire, we are in very great danger!"

Answers to Comprehension Questions

1 Modestus was terrified and hid (because he knew Salvius). Strythio was braver, and walked up to Salvius, offering him assistance.
2 Salvius wanted Strythio to take him to headquarters.
3 He worried that, if the centurion Valerius was at the headquarters building, he would arrest him (Strythio) the moment he saw him.
4 He said that Modestus' main job was repairing buildings, and that is what he was doing there.
5 Modestus suggested it was probably his brother whom Salvius had seen in Aquae Sulis. His brother was a very sick man (and presumably often visited the healing baths).

6 He took him toward the granaries.
7 He said that the buildings did look like granaries. The headquarters were built that way to fool the Britons, who often attacked the camp with the intention of setting fire to headquarters. If headquarters was disguised as granaries, the buildings would be safer.
8 Strythio saw the centurion Valerius coming out of the real headquarters.

The story in 25.1 will make better sense if students have read 22.1. It may also help if they have not read 22.3, 23.1 or 24.1.

26.1 Agricola and the Emperor

I

Agricola was sitting alone in the headquarters, thinking over Salvius' words. He was very disturbed, because he did not know whether this Roman senator was speaking the truth.

"I don't trust that Salvius," he said to himself. "For he is not a very trustworthy man. However, the Emperor Domitian sent him to Britain to inspect...and to seize?...Cogidubnus' kingdom. I must be careful, because a new emperor who trusts this kind of man is either crazy or evil."

II

Agricola, having said these words to himself, decided to write a letter to send to the emperor:

"Gnaeus Julius Agricola, governor of the imperial province, sends greetings to Emperor Domitian Augustus, son of the Divine Vespasian.

"I am happy, sir, that I am bringing you excellent victories, worthy of your name. Your father, Vespasian, sent me to this island to impose peace on the

80

Britons. After I had looked after the administration of Britain for five years, I was able to occupy the whole island except Caledonia (Scotland). Therefore I had to wage war against the Caledonians. I sent out ships to scout the harbors of the barbarians; at the same time I myself proceeded to Caledonia with many soldiers.

"The Caledonians are the most courageous of all the Britons. However, although they resisted bravely and, having entered our camp at night, killed many Romans, we were finally able to defeat them. A few fled; they burned their homes and killed their wives and children, because they did not want them to be slaves. The next day, we were able to find no barbarians except dead ones.

"I decided to announce this victory to you so that you could rejoice with us. Your soldiers, Roman soldiers, now occupy all of Britain!"

Answers to Comprehension Questions

1 Agricola's own title (**lēgātus Augustī prōpraetor**) reminds the emperor of the authority he has to act on behalf of the emperor. Using both **Imperātor** and **Augustus** in Domitian's title is an indication that Agricola in turn recognizes the emperor's authority. The phrase **Dīvī Vespasiānī fīliō** both accepts the state religious belief in the divinity of deceased emperors (Domitian will not be able to accuse him of disloyalty) and reminds Domitian (as does the next paragraph) that his father appointed Agricola to his post.

2 This is a kind of flattery, saying that the victories are **optimās** and therefore worthy of the name of the emperor. Agricola's hope is that the emperor will thus approve of his actions and, since Agricola now appears to have some doubt about the emperor's character, will not be inclined to think or act unfavorably towards the governor.

3 His mandate was to impose peace on the island.

4 Caledonia was the one area of the island which had not been satisfactorily subdued.

5 He sent out ships to scout the Caledonians' harbors.

6 The Caledonians made a night attack on the Roman camp and killed many soldiers.

7 They burned their houses and killed their wives and children.

8 They did not wish their wives and children to become slaves to the Romans.

26.2 Vincens (Vincent)

I

Agricola was having a talk with Silanus, the commander of the legion, and with the tribunes. For these men, soldiers of the highest authority, had assembled in the headquarters to talk about Vincent, a new soldier. Silanus, holding a letter, explained to Agricola why he had summoned him to this meeting:

"When Vincent arrived at this camp, he usually delighted us very much. For, when he was sent to war, he always fought bravely. Yesterday, however, Rufus, a very trustworthy tribune, came into the headquarters and showed me this letter, written by a friend. Look at these words: 'Vincent is a slave. Do not keep a slave in the army!' What are we going to do? We must decide."

II

When Agricola had read the letter intently, he thought the matter over. Then he pronounced his judgment:

"If these words are true, Vincent must return to Italy. It is not proper for slaves to fight in the army. Call the young man to headquarters at once!"

The tribune Rufus left to find the soldier. Vincent, summoned to headquarters, obeyed these orders eagerly. He wondered whether the commander had decided to give him a reward, because he had fought so bravely. However, when he caught sight of the serious faces of the commander and the tribunes, he quickly became worried.

Agricola, showing Vincent the letter, asked,

"Do you see these words? Are these words true?"

"I don't understand Latin well," replied the young man. "Read the words to me!"

"If you don't understand Latin well," said Agricola, "these words are indeed true. You are a slave."

"Who told you this?" shouted Vincent. "Did the other soldiers betray me? Many of the soldiers are jealous of me, because I am a very brave and very enthusiastic soldier! It's not fair!"

Then the young man began to cry.

Agricola, ignoring the tears, gave Vincent these orders:

"You must go back to the barracks and prepare to leave the camp. I have to punish those who ignore the orders of the emperor; you have to obey my orders."

This story was based on an unhappy incident. Vincent, a popular student who no longer lived in our school district, tried to hide the situation by using his grandparents' address. When his stratagem was revealed, he was forced to transfer out of our school, with tears all round. The story used an incident familiar to his fellow-students to illustrate the similar rule that slaves were not permitted to enlist in the Roman army. The transliterated name "Vincens" is appropriate for the character's heroism in battle.

Answers to Comprehension Questions

1 Vincent would have to go back to Italy.
2 It was not proper for slaves to serve in the army.
3 He thought he might be in line for a reward because he had fought so bravely.
4 The faces of the commander and the tribunes were grave.
5 He said that he couldn't read the words in the letter because he didn't understand Latin well.
6 To Agricola Vincent's admission of illiteracy in Latin was strong proof that he was indeed a slave.
7 He suggested the other soldiers had given him away because they were jealous of his bravery and enthusiasm.
8 He told him to return to barracks and prepare to leave the camp.
9 He had to enforce the rules/commands of the emperor.

26.3 Quintus Prepares to Leave

I

When Quintus heard about the death of Cogidubnus, he hurried to the headquarters to look for Rufus. There the military tribune was having a conversation with Agricola about the dead king. After entering headquarters, Quintus greeted the commander and the tribune.

"Greetings, friends! Are you also very sad because a very loyal man has died? We Romans must never forget this good friend.

"But now I have to return to Italy. Your father, Rufus, sent me to this island in order to find you. This I have now done. Dumnorix sent me to this camp in order to help Cogidubnus. This I can no longer do. It is dangerous for me to stay in Britain, because Salvius, a man of evil character, wants to punish me."

When Agricola and Rufus found out what Quintus wanted to do, they promised him help.

II

Quintus had decided to travel to the city of Rome in order to have a talk with the emperor. He explained his plan to Rufus:

"I don't trust that Salvius. Surely Domitian did not want to seize Cogidubnus' kingdom? Surely I can tell the whole story to the emperor? Salvius must be punished. Only the emperor can look after this kind of situation. And so I must hurry to the City."

Rufus replied, "Although you don't trust Salvius, you should also be wary of Domitian. For Cogidubnus was a friend of Claudius, a friend of Vespasian, but not Domitian's friend. The new emperor favors younger men; perhaps Salvius is one of these young men. If Salvius is speaking the truth, you must be careful."

When Rufus was saying these words, Agricola came back into the headquarters and announced,

"I have given orders to Valerius, an excellent centurion. He has prepared a horse; in this way you can ride quickly to the coast. He has also looked for guards; they can take you along the dangerous roads. He had two brave soldiers who were guarding the prison; but, although he has looked for these soldiers, he can't find them. You must stay here until Valerius can find them; then you can proceed to Italy safely."

Answers to Comprehension Questions

1 a He couldn't believe that Domitian really wanted to seize Cogidubnus' kingdom.
   b He hoped to be able to tell the whole story to the emperor.

   c The emperor was the only one who could handle this situation.
2 a The leaders who favored Cogidubnus were now gone. Perhaps the new emperor favored younger men like Salvius.
   b He told him he should be wary of the emperor.
3 a He had arranged for a horse, so that he could travel more quickly to the coast.
   b He was trying to get guards to accompany Quintus on his journey.
   c They might have been Modestus and Strythio.
   d He suggested Quintus needed to wait for these guards, to guarantee his safety. From what we know of those two, their presence would do anything but!

26.4 Rufus Astonished

I

After Rufus left headquarters he hurried to the hospital. For the doctor whom Agricola had summoned had sent Quintus there so that he could care for his wound. When the tribune entered the hospital, he caught sight of the young man lying on a bed near the window. He moved forward to the bed and prepared to ask why Quintus had come to the camp wounded and filthy. Quintus, however, wondered whether this soldier was going to believe him. For a short time they both inspected each other and said nothing.

II

Rufus was the first to speak. "Hello! I am Rufus, a Roman tribune. Agricola sent me to you to find out as much as possible about you. For Agricola..."

Suddenly Quintus exclaimed, "Rufus? Tell me, where did you live before you began military service?"

Rufus, hesitating, replied, "In Alexandria. Why do you ask?"

"Was your father's name Barbillus?"

"Yes! How do you know this? What have you heard about my father?"

By now very excited, Rufus began to question Quintus. He, however, lifting a finger to his lip(s), pointed out the letter lying on a table. Rufus snatched the letter and read it through eagerly. At first he was so moved that he couldn't say anything. Then, almost in tears, he said,

"Friend, I thank you very much because you showed so many kindnesses to my father. You are indeed a man of the utmost virtue. Now I must return to headquarters and tell Agricola everything I know about Quintus Caecilius Iucundus!"

After Rufus said this, he left the hospital as quickly as possible in order to inform Agricola.

Answers to Comprehension Questions

1 He had been sent by Agricola to find out as much as possible about Quintus.
2 When he heard the name "Rufus," he had to find out if this was the man he was looking for.
3 He asked him where he lived before joining the army and he asked if his father's name was Barbillus.
4 He wondered how Quintus could have known that and what Quintus knew about his father.
5 He was probably still very weak and the letter could tell what he needed to tell. The letter in Barbillus' handwriting would also help support Quintus' story.
6 He was so moved that he couldn't speak.
7 He had to go and tell Agricola all he had learned about Quintus.

84

27.1 Salvius and the Guards

I

After Agricola heard about the death of Cogidubnus, he dismissed Salvius at once. The latter, after leaving headquarters, thought to himself,

"I have to hurry to Cogidubnus' palace. I want to find out about Cogidubnus' will."

Salvius had to have horses and guards in order to travel to the king's palace. However, he didn't want to disclose to Agricola where he was hurrying. Therefore, he adopted the following plan:

He stayed in his room for three hours. Then, when it was getting dark, he went secretly to the centurion Valerius. Valerius, who did not know about Cogidubnus' death, trusted Salvius. He was so eager to help that he gave him two excellent guards: Modestus and Strythio!

II

Salvius with the two guards was riding through the darkness towards Cogidubnus' palace. Because Modestus recognized Salvius, he was terrified. He wondered whether Salvius was going to recognize him. For Salvius had seen him in the temple at Aquae Sulis. However, because Salvius could not see the guards through the darkness, and because he was thinking only about Cogidubnus, he did not recognize Modestus.

After a few hours, they came to a deep river. Salvius asked the guards where the bridge was.

Strythio replied, "The bridge which used to stand here was half-collapsed. A heavy weight destroyed it." Then he looked intently at Modestus.

Because Salvius wanted to reach the palace as quickly as possible, he ordered the guards to find out where they could cross the river. The two soldiers went off into the woods and soon reported back,

"It is easy for us to cross this river. Near those trees there are many rocks in the water. Using these rocks, we can reach the other bank."

The guards led Salvius to the rocks. He ordered Strythio to cross first. Strythio, however, was so timid that he refused. Modestus also was unwilling. Salvius, therefore, after cursing the cowardice of the guards, began to cross. Suddenly his horse slipped on a rock and threw Salvius into the water. From the midst of the waves, he shouted,

"Blockheads! Help me!"

But the blockheads were not so stupid that they stayed there. They fled into the woods as quickly as possible.

When Salvius had dragged himself, soaked through, from the water, he proceeded to the palace alone.

Answers to Comprehension Questions

1 He recognized Salvius and was worried that Salvius would recognize him.
2 Salvius had seen Modestus in the temple at Aquae Sulis (Bath).
3 It was dark, and Salvius' thoughts were elsewhere (on Cogidubnus).
4 They reached a deep river, with no bridge across it.
5 The bridge that used to be there was rickety and had been destroyed by a heavy weight.
6 He ordered the soldiers to find a place to cross the river.
7 There was a place nearby where they could use the rocks in the river to make their way across.
8 His horse slipped on a rock and threw Salvius into the water.
9 They ran off into the woods.
10 He had to carry on alone (and soaked through).

Portions of the story in 27.1 will make more sense if students have read 23.1.

27.2 A Very Wretched Soldier

I

Modestus, a very wretched soldier, was sitting in the prison. For the commander had ordered him to guard the prison. While he was sitting there, he thought to himself,

"Why do I have to stay here? I hate this life. (This life is hateful to me.) When I am guarding the prison I can neither eat food nor play dice nor visit beautiful girls."

When he had said these words to himself, he was so upset that he decided to undertake a bold plan. He wanted to invite his friends to the prison to play dice. However, because he did not know how he could undertake such a major plan, he had to consult Strythio.

When Strythio was summoned to the prison, he hurried as quickly as he could in order to help his friend.

II

After Strythio entered the prison, he listened to Modestus' plan. However, when he found out what his friend had in mind, he laughed loudly:

"Nothing is easier! Many cells are deserted, where we can bring dice, food...even girls. Don't be afraid! I can look after everything."

Having said these words, Strythio hurried out of the prison to carry out Modestus' instructions.

The next day, while Modestus was waiting for his friends, Valerius, the centurion, entered the prison to inspect the cells and the prisoners. Although Modestus wanted to stand near the door to warn his friends, the centurion asked that he show the cells to him. When they had reached the last cell, suddenly Strythio, the friends, and even the girls hurried through the door, carrying food and making a lot of noise. Then, when they caught sight of Valerius, they halted, terrified.

Valerius immediately asked Modestus why these friends had come to the prison:

"Surely you are not playing dice again? It is not proper for Roman soldiers to play dice in a prison."

"Oh no, my dear centurion," replied Modestus. "These friends came so that...so that..."

"So that we could give Modestus congratulations," shouted Strythio, who had had a clever idea. "Nigrina, the British dancing-girl, wants to marry Modestus. We to Modestus congratulations..."

"What?" asked Modestus, thunderstruck. (Modestus did not want to have any wife!)

But the centurion, who had understood the situation well, also congratulated Modestus and Nigrina (who was there), and ordered Strythio and his friends to eat the food, to play dice...and to summon a priest to consecrate the marriage. Again Modestus was a very wretched soldier!

Answers to Comprehension Questions

1 They could use an empty cell (or cells) for their partying and dice-playing. He would look after everything.
2 The centurion Valerius came to inspect the prison.
3 He wanted to stand near the door to warn off his friends.
4 Valerius asked Modestus to give him a personal tour of the cells.
5 Just as they reached the last cell, Strythio, the friends and even the girls burst into the prison, carrying food and making a lot of noise.
6 He suspected that Modestus and his friends were wanting to play dice again.

7 Strythio said the group had come to celebrate and congratulate Modestus because the dancing-girl, Nigrina, wanted to marry him.
8 He had no wish to marry anyone.
9 He told the group to summon a priest in order to consecrate the marriage.

Students who are familiar with the musical Guys and Dolls *will notice a similarity between the plot twist here and the fate of Nathan Detroit.*

27.3 Happy Prisoners

I

After Modestus was put in charge of the prison, he was so upset that he didn't know what he should do. He wondered why the commander had given him this 'reward.' When he was thinking this over (to himself), he suddenly had a clever idea. Leaving the prison, he hurried to headquarters and asked Silanus to send Strythio to the prison as well, in order to help him.

"Strythio," said Modestus, "is a very reliable soldier. You must give him the same reward."

"My dear Modestus," replied Silanus, "few of my soldiers are braver than you. I am happy to listen to your wishes. You must hurry to your friend. Give him my instructions! Look after the prison well!"

After the commander had said these words, he left to inspect the rest of the soldiers, and Modestus left to look for his comrade.

II

Modestus and Strythio, while managing the prison, were in the habit of having conversations with each other. One day, when they were talking about the prisoners, Modestus asked why they were so unhappy that they were always trying to escape.

"Happy prisoners don't want to escape," he said to Strythio. "How can we make these prisoners happy?"

"A prisoner whose cell is beautiful should obviously be happy," replied Strythio. "The prisoners need to paint the cells and decorate them with garlands of roses."

But when the friends ordered the prisoners to do this, they threw the roses on the floor and the paint into the guards' faces!

Then Strythio proposed another plan:

"A prisoner to whom we have given too little pleasure is obviously unhappy. We should invite Nigrina from the town to the prison. A dancing-girl always pleases prisoners."

And so Nigrina, summoned by the friends, hurried to the prison to dance for the prisoners. However, before she began to dance, Modestus decided to tell a few jokes. The jokes were so stupid and the shouting of the prisoners so raucous that Modestus had to shut up and Nigrina had to flee in tears.

Finally, Strythio had his best idea (an excellent idea):

"These cells are dark. A prisoner who remains in the dark all day cannot be happy."

And so the comrades began to knock down a wall of the prison in order to make the windows larger. But the prisoners, seizing this opportunity, very happily burst out through the new openings. When Modestus noticed this, he said,

"Oh dear! Now the prisoners are happy, but we are very unhappy. Again, we must run away!"

Answers to Comprehension Questions

1 His plans were all designed to make the prisoners happy.
2 Happy prisoners would not keep trying to escape.

3 a The first plan tried to deal with jail cells that were not attractive. The second tried to deal with lives that were too dull and unpleasant in prison.
   b The first plan envisaged the prisoners painting and decorating their cells. The second plan had Nigrina coming from town to dance for the prisoners.
   c The first plan failed because the prisoners were unwilling to do the painting and decorating. (They threw the decorations on the floor and they threw the paint at the guards.) The second plan failed because Modestus decided to tell some pretty weak jokes before introducing Nigrina, and the prisoners rioted in reaction to them (forcing Modestus to stop and Nigrina to flee in tears).
4 a The third plan was to knock down a wall of the prison to enlarge the windows.
   b The prison was too dark, in Strythio's opinion, for prisoners to be happy.
   c The prisoners eagerly escaped through the new holes in the wall created by the renovations.
5 Ironically, Modestus and Strythio did make the prisoners happy! (And, as an extra bonus, they would no longer be trying to escape, since they had already succeeded!)

28.1 Rufilla's Sadness

I

When Salvius had traveled through Britain for many days, extorting money and riches, he finally returned to the palace. He was so tired that he hurried to his bedroom, because he wanted to sleep. However, he was met by his wife, Rufilla, upset with anger and sadness. She entered the bedroom with her husband and asked him why he had deserted her.

Salvius, astonished by these words, ordered Rufilla to be silent:

"It is not proper for you to curse your husband in this way. You must return to your bedroom."

II

Rufilla, however, refused to leave the bedroom.

"It pleases you," she said, "to travel through the province; it does not please you to take your wife with you. You leave me alone in this palace, which is buffeted by cold winds and filled with strange voices!

"While you were away, I could not sleep, because dreadful dreams frightened me. The ghost of King Cogidubnus was walking through the bedroom, shaking his blood-stained hands. The king kept asking why Salvius had killed him. When I got up to wash the king's hands, the ghost vanished. O Salvius! Why was I not able to wash those blood-stained hands?"

Then Rufilla, begging her husband to sell the palace and go back to Italy, burst into tears. Salvius, upset by his wife's fear, did not know what he should say. Suddenly a messenger entered the bedroom and handed Salvius a letter written by the emperor. The emperor had ordered Salvius to return to the city of Rome.

Answers to Comprehension Questions

1 She suggested he should have taken her with him.
2 It was buffeted by cold winds and filled with strange voices.
3 The ghost of King Cogidubnus walked through the bedroom, shaking his

blood-stained hands and asking why Salvius had killed him.
4 She tried to wash the king's hands.
5 The ghost vanished.
6 She begged him to sell the palace and return to Italy.
7 He was so upset by her fear that he didn't know what he should say.
8 The message was an order from the emperor for Salvius to return to the city of Rome.

Students who know Shakespeare's play Macbeth *will see a certain similarity between Rufilla's plight and that of Lady Macbeth.*

28.2 Modestus, the Athlete

I

Gaius Julius Silanus, the commander of the Second Legion, was walking through the streets of the camp in order to inspect all the buildings. When he had reached the prison, he heard loud shouts. So great was the noise that Silanus hurried at once to the prison gate. For he wanted to find out what was happening. After entering the prison, he ordered the prisoners to be quiet. When they had done this, the commander approached the first cell to ask the prisoner why everyone was shouting. Overcome with fear, the prisoner pointed his hands to the wall and whispered, "The discus...the discus..." He could not say anything else.

Silanus, suspecting a plot, decided to ask the other Britons the same thing. While he was doing this, he suddenly heard a terrifying sound. Something had struck the prison wall. At once, the prisoners began to shout again.

The commander, angered by the noise, ran into the courtyard to find out what had struck the wall. In the middle of the courtyard, he recognized two soldiers, Modestus and Strythio.

II

Strythio was handing Modestus a discus. Then Modestus stepped forward to throw it. Suddenly catching sight of the commander, he let the discus fall to the ground. He was so surprised that he stood there motionless.

Silanus walked up to the soldiers and angrily asked what they were doing.

"I put you in charge of the prison," he shouted. "Why aren't you guarding the prisoners? Why are you throwing the discus in the courtyard? Why are you frightening the prisoners?"

Strythio replied,

"My friend, Modestus, is a very famous athlete. He can throw the discus a long way. This year the Olympic Games are taking place in Greece. Modestus was practicing so that he could win first prize. We have to go off to Greece!"

"Blockheads!" shouted the commander. "Roman soldiers don't compete in the Olympic Games. People who are in the army in Britain don't go off to Greece. You'd better go back to the prison."

Suddenly everyone heard a loud uproar from the prison. Vercobrix, the son of a British chieftain, was trying to escape again. He had attacked a guard and was now running through the open gate. Silanus, noticing this, rushed through the courtyard at once. Modestus, however, picked up his discus and heaved it energetically. The discus flew far through the air and hit...Silanus! As the commander lay unconscious on the ground, Strythio turned to Modestus and said,

"My friend, we'd better not practice the discus any longer. Now we had better practice racing! We have to flee as quickly as possible!"

The two soldiers made an immediate exit.

Answers to Comprehension Questions

1 Strythio was handing Modestus a discus and Modestus was getting ready to throw it.
2 They were supposed to be guarding the prison, not practicing the discus and frightening the prisoners.
3 The Olympic Games were to be held that year. Modestus was an excellent discus thrower and he was practicing so that he could win first prize.
4 He told them that Roman soldiers didn't compete in the Olympics and that people stationed in Britain certainly wouldn't be going off to Greece for the competitions.
5 Vercobrix, the son of a British chieftain, was trying to escape again.
6 He threw his discus to try to stop Vercobrix but hit Silanus instead.
7 They had to take up racing!

30.1 Among the Tombs

I

In the middle of the night, a young man was walking very carefully towards the city of Rome. His horse and his friends had been left at a near-by inn so that the young man could approach the city alone. Suddenly, as he was going past a cemetery (past tombs), he caught sight of a person standing near a large tomb. The young man was forced to stop.

"I must be careful," he said to himself. "Unless I am deceived, this man is affected too much by a love of tombs. I should avoid such men."

Then he started looking for a place to hide (where he could hide), from where he could watch the man secretly. For he wanted to learn what he was doing there.

Suddenly the man caught sight of the young man and shouted in astonishment,

"Who are you? Who sent you? Why was I being watched?"

II

"I am a stranger," said the young man, "and I have never visited the city of Rome before. I don't want to harm you. However, tell me! Why are you attracted by these tombs? Surely you are not looking for ghosts?"

"No," replied the other. "But one day my ghost is going to live here. I am Quintus Haterius Latronianus, a very well-known contractor. Perhaps you have seen my buildings: the Flavian Amphitheater, the new arch...but you are a stranger! Of course you haven't seen these buildings. I must show them to you...in the morning! But meanwhile, look at these tombs! Surely they are very beautiful?"

The young man, who did not know whether he wanted to speak with a contractor who loved tombs, nevertheless agreed.

"My patron," said Haterius, "sold me this little plot of land, where I could build tombs for myself and my family. Here I intend to sculpt my name and my buildings on a tomb and in this way make my deeds known. My patron is a generous man, isn't he?"

"How many sesterces did you give your patron when this plot of land was sold?" asked the young man.

"Just three million sesterces," replied Haterius.

"Ye gods!" shouted the young man. "Your patron is a thief! But my friends warned me not to buy anything in Rome. In the town of Pompeii..."

"Are you a Pompeian?" exclaimed the contractor. "I knew a Pompeian merchant, named Lucius Caecilius Iucundus."

"I am his son," replied the young man, "Quintus Caecilius Iucundus. I must..."

"You must stay at my house," replied Haterius. "And tomorrow I want to show you my buildings and my patron!"

Answers to Comprehension Questions

1 He wanted to know why he was attracted to these tombs.
2 He said that one day his ghost would be living there.
3 He promised to show him some of the buildings he had constructed in Rome.
4 He wasn't sure he wanted to continue talking to a tomb-lover.
5 He was going to sculpt his name and his buildings on a family tomb so that his deeds would be known to posterity.
6 His patron had sold him the site.
7 He felt that Haterius had been robbed.
8 He invited Quintus to stay at his home.
9 One reason would have been the connection he had made with Quintus' father. Another could simply be vanity: the chance to show off his building projects.
10 Haterius' patron was Salvius, someone whom Quintus would probably not want to meet at this point.

30.2 Haterius Gives Thanks

I

Quintus Haterius Latronianus, overcome with joy, was looking for his wife in the house. For a messenger had been sent to the house to invite the contractor to the emperor's palace. Haterius had been asked by Domitian to repair the Temple of Jupiter Capitolinus. He was holding in his hand a letter written by the emperor.

"Today we are being honored because of the magnificent arch," he said to himself. "Domitian was obviously pleased by the arch."

Then, catching sight of Vitellia, he explained the whole story. She replied:

"You must thank Salvius profusely, because you have been given such a great project, such great prestige, and such great riches."

II

That night, Haterius was sleeping soundly in his bedroom. In a dream the new temple was being built; huge columns, made of marble, were being constructed; a gilded roof was being placed on top of the temple. The emperor, Salvius and very many senators had come to praise the great project. Domitian approached Haterius to announce to him:

"Quintus Haterius Latronianus, today you are being made a priest by order of the emperor."

While Haterius was thinking over these words, suddenly the ground began to tremble. Huge blocks of marble were falling to the ground. Many senators were being killed by these blocks; the shouts of the others were being raised to the sky. Haterius stood there motionless. Suddenly a dreadful voice was heard:

"Alas for you, Haterius! You gave thanks to the emperor and to Salvius; however, you overlooked the one whose temple you are building. You must not overlook Jupiter the Best and the Greatest. Beware! Beware!..."

Haterius was suddenly awakened. Overcome with panic, he hurried to the Temple of Jupiter in the middle of the night and, praying to the god, made a sacrifice.

Answers to Comprehension Questions

1   Huge columns made of marble were being constructed; a gilded roof was being placed on the top of the new temple. The emperor, Salvius and many senators were on hand to praise the project. (*any two*)

2   He announced to Haterius that he was being made a priest that day.

3   The earth shook; huge blocks of marble began falling to the ground; many senators were being killed by these falling materials; the screaming of the rest of the people was being raised to the sky. (*any two*)

4   The voice suggested that Haterius had thanked the emperor and Salvius but had forgotten to thank the one whose temple was being built. Haterius was warned not to overlook Jupiter.

5   He ran to the Temple of Jupiter at once (in the middle of the night), prayed to the god, and made a sacrifice.

30.3   A Sacrifice

I

Gaius Salvius Liberalis was meeting with a few friends in a sacred shrine which had been built in a grove near the city of Rome. These friends, who had been named priests of the Arval Brotherhood (Brothers) by the emperor, usually made sacrifices at the first hour of daylight. Therefore, influenced by hope of Domitian's favor, they were consulting each other about a sacrifice for the emperor's safety.

"Comrades!" said Salvius. "The emperor is surrounded by enemies. We are rightly praised because of our loyalty. Therefore it is fitting for us, who have been put in charge of these sacrifices, to choose a victim."

II

The next day, this victim, a white cow, was being led by slaves through the streets of the City. Suddenly a dreadful thing happened. For a girl, who was being chased by three boys, burst into the middle of the street. Unaware of the danger, she did not see the slaves and the cow, nor they her; she slipped under the cow's foot and was seriously injured. Almost unconscious from pain, she cried out in such a loud voice that a crowd of citizens, attracted by the din, hurried to this part of the street. The girl's sister, affected by her panic and pain, was on hand to help her.

"Although you are in pain and terrified," she said, "you must be brave. Do not give up hope! Do not die!"

Meanwhile, Salvius was marching ahead of the procession and had not seen what had happened. When he heard the shouting, he hurried towards it; there he caught sight of the girl and her sister lying in the street and the crowd standing around. After the slaves had told about the girl, Salvius drew his sword and stabbed her.

"This girl has offended the gods; therefore she must die," he explained.

Then he departed with the slaves and the cow and left the crowd standing astonished in the street.

Answers to Comprehension Questions

1 A white cow was being led through the streets of Rome as a sacrifice victim. Suddenly a girl, who was being chased by three boys, ran out into the street. She didn't see the procession nor did the procession see her. She fell under the cow's foot and was badly injured. (any three details)
2 The girl was screaming from pain.
3 Her sister was trying to comfort her (telling her to be brave, not to despair and not to die).
4 Salvius was marching at the head of the procession.

5 He heard the screams of the girl (and perhaps also the shouting of the arriving spectators).
6 He drew his sword and stabbed the girl.
7 He said she had offended the gods and had to die.

30.4 The Sisters Warn Haterius

I

Rufilla, Salvius' wife, was sitting in the garden. Suddenly Vitellia, Haterius' wife, and Rufilla's sister, was brought into the garden by a slave. Rufilla was so happy when she saw Vitellia that she embraced her sister and asked her to sit down beside her. Then the slave was sent into the house to bring goblets of wine.

"I am really delighted at your arrival, my dear Vitellia," said Rufilla. "Because we are always being deserted by our husbands, we should visit each other more often. Is Haterius well?"

"My husband is a man of very little common sense," replied Vitellia. "When the Arch of Titus was being built, he worked too hard, in hope of Domitian's favor. Now he is overcome by pain and anger because the emperor himself has not thanked him. I am tired of his complaints."

II

After Vitellia had found fault with her husband in this way, the two women reflected together on how they could warn Haterius. For it was dangerous to criticize Emperor Domitian. Vitellia, therefore, overcome with fear, had been compelled to visit her sister in order to seek help.

Suddenly Rufilla asked where Haterius was at that moment.

"He is working at the construction site with his workmen," replied Vitellia. "Why do you ask?"

"We must send a messenger to the work site," said Rufilla. "This messenger can hand Haterius a letter written like this..." and Rufilla began to put together the words:

"Beware, Haterius! The emperor is pleased to give a well-deserved reward to those whom he likes...and whom he hates. Do not offend the emperor!"

This letter, written quickly, was given to a slave, for him to take to Haterius. The slave, who had not been informed what warning was in the letter nor who had written it, hurried to the building site to find Haterius. He caught sight of him in the middle of the site, urging on his workers...and muttering about the emperor. But when he had read the letter, he immediately grew pale and sat down slowly on a block of marble...

Afterwards, nothing further was said at Haterius' house about the emperor!

Answers to Comprehension Questions

1 They felt it was dangerous to criticize Emperor Domitian.
2 They should send it to Haterius at the construction site.
3 She said that Domitian gave well-deserved rewards to those he liked and to those he hated (implying an unpleasant fate for those he hated); so Haterius should avoid offending the emperor.
4 He was not told the contents or the author(s) of the letter.
5 He was at the work site urging on his workers and muttering about the emperor.
6 He grew pale and had to sit down on a block of marble.
7 There was no further mention of the emperor at Haterius' house.

31.1 A City of Barbarians

I

After Euphrosyne and her slave had been driven away from Haterius' house, they proceeded through the streets of the City to find a place to live. Although the slave had been advised not to give up hope, he wondered why they had come to this unfriendly city. For everywhere, when they looked for lodgings, they were rejected by haughty masters. Finally, after finding no suitable place, the slave said,

"Mistress, we must leave this city. For here we are laughed at, I am thrown in the mud, and you are greeted with insults. Rome is a city of barbarians!"

After he had said these words, the slave picked up their luggage onto his shoulders in order to return to the harbor.

II

However, it was difficult to hurry to the harbor, because a huge mob, which blocked their way, was filling the streets. This crowd was all hurrying in the same direction. When Euphrosyne noticed this, she asked her slave where these Romans were hurrying. Because he was also astonished by the noise of the citizens, he shouted to a passing merchant,

"Friend! Where is this crowd hurrying?"

"Don't you know?" replied the other. "Today the emperor has announced magnificent games. We are all hurrying to the new amphitheater, where a splendid show is being presented."

Then he continued to run through the streets.

Euphrosyne, overcome with doubt, was not able to understand these words. For she had neither heard of the amphitheater nor seen any shows. Therefore, the slave had to explain this:

"In the amphitheater, gladiators fight, armed men who try to kill animals, prisoners, and other gladiators. The winning gladiators are given fame, money, even freedom; the losing gladiators are given death!"

Euphrosyne, astonished by these words, became pale.

"Surely the Roman citizens are not hurrying to a slaughter?" she asked. "Surely they don't want to watch men killing other men?"

"Yes," replied the slave.

When Euphrosyne heard this (these words), she shouted,

"Rome is a city of barbarians!"

Then she lifted their luggage onto the slave's shoulders and hurried to the harbor.

Answers to Comprehension Questions

1 They could not travel quickly to the harbor because a huge crowd was blocking the way.
2 Everyone was hurrying in the same direction.
3 He asked a passing merchant where everyone was headed.
4 He was told that they were all hurrying to the new amphitheater where the emperor was putting on a magnificent show.
5 She had never heard of the amphitheater and had never seen a show.
6 He explained that gladiators, who were armed men, fought with animals, prisoners, or other gladiators. The winners gained fame, money, and even freedom. The losers died.
7 She could not believe that Romans would be hurrying so eagerly to a slaughter, to see men killing other men.
8 It was a city of barbarians.

32.1 The River Tiber

I

It was night. Near the city of Rome, a young man, accompanied by a few slaves, was riding along the Via Flaminia. He was proceeding slowly so that he would not awaken the citizens who lived near the road. His slaves had also been warned to proceed very carefully. Therefore, they followed their master, examining the woods, the fields, and even the passers-by.

Finally they reached the Mulvian Bridge, where the young man, although he was worn out from travel and lack of sleep, silently laughed.

"I am now entering the city of Rome," he thought to himself, "where Gaius Salvius Liberalis lives, the man whom I must punish...and whom I am going to punish!"

II

This young man was Quintus Caecilius Iucundus. He had left Britain very quickly after the death of Cogidubnus and had wandered through many countries for ten months. For, influenced by fear of Salvius, he had not dared to head straight for Rome. Now at last, having endured many dangers, he had reached the City itself.

He was in such a happy frame of mind when he thought about his arrival that he walked to the middle of the bridge and suddenly flung himself into the river. The slaves, who watched their master swimming with astonishment, were completely unaware of why he was doing this. However, when he caught sight of their astonishment (them astonished), he shouted,

"Don't be worried, my comrades! This very famous river flows through the city of Rome. Into this river angry citizens often throw statues of their enemies. Into this river they sometimes throw the enemies themselves!

"I consider Salvius such an enemy. I want to tell other Romans about his crimes. One day these citizens are going to throw Salvius' statue, or Salvius himself, into the Tiber. I am swimming in the river of my own accord; having done this, I can warn Salvius about the coldness of the water!"

Answers to Comprehension Questions

1 It had taken him ten months.
2 He was afraid of Salvius and had not dared to head straight for the city.
3 He went out to the center of the Mulvian Bridge and jumped down into the river.
4 They were dumbfounded and could not figure out why he was doing this.
5 Angry citizens often threw statues of their enemies, or even the enemies themselves, into the Tiber.
6 He hoped that by telling other Romans about Salvius' crimes, he would get them to do the same to Salvius.
7 He would be in a position to warn Salvius about the water temperature!

32.2 A Dream Explained

I

It was night. Quintus Haterius Latronianus was walking anxiously in the garden. For a dreadful event, seen in a dream, had so frightened him that he could not sleep. In the middle of the night he had left his bedroom to think things over, but he was completely at a loss as to what he should do.

While Haterius was sitting on a chair for a short time, Vitellia approached her husband, who was deep in thought. For when Haterius left the house, she had decided to find out where he was going, why he could not sleep, and what he was going to do next.

When Haterius saw his wife, he tried to hide his anxiety. However, she persuaded him with gentle words to tell the whole story. When he had done this, Haterius returned to the house in a calmer frame of mind.

II

The next day, Vitellia spoke to her husband about the dream in this way:

"You must go to Salvius. For his friend, the philosopher Athenodorus, understands dreams. This philosopher, after hearing your dream, can explain it to you."

Haterius, won over by these words of his wife, headed to Salvius. By chance, he was being visited by Athenodorus, to whom Haterius told his dream in this way:

"In the dream, the Emperor Domitian ordered me to build a magnificent palace. And so I obeyed the emperor very quickly. But the palace, which had been built so quickly, was destroyed just as quickly. In one night the walls, the roof, the whole palace fell to the ground! I was cursed by the emperor; I was led to prison, where guards were going to kill me. Suddenly I was awakened. Now can you understand my anxiety?"

Athenodorus, however, replied in a steady voice:

"Some people have dreams which mean the opposite. Don't be worried. I promise you a magnificent palace, a large reward given by the emperor...and a long life!"

Haterius returned home with relieved spirits.

Answers to Comprehension Questions

1. Salvius had a friend, the philosopher Athenodorus, who could interpret dreams.
2. Athenodorus was visiting Salvius at the time.
3. He asked Haterius to build a magnificent palace.
4. In one night it was destroyed. The walls, the roof, the whole palace fell to the ground.
5. The emperor imprisoned Haterius and apparently ordered the death penalty.
6. He said it meant the opposite of what it seemed. He promised Haterius a magnificent palace, a large reward and a long life.
7. Haterius went home with his spirits lightened.

32.3 Haterius' Revenge

I

After the rowdy dinner, Eryllus, Haterius' judge of good taste, was very frightened. For, since the dining-room had been destroyed by the guests and the philosopher had gone back to Greece, he was wondering whether Haterius was going to dismiss him.

"I must avoid the master," he thought to himself. "I am forced into finding a new plan."

As Eryllus was thinking this over, Haterius himself burst through the doorway, very upset. Although Eryllus kept trying to soothe his anger and, pouring out tears, kept begging him not to punish him, he (Haterius) was not influenced by these words.

II

"Blockhead!" shouted the patron angrily. "Thanks to you, I am now the laughing-stock of Rome. Sabinus, a consul of the highest authority, whose favor I was trying to court, now despises me. How can I attain the highest honors if the consul despises me? I am now mocked by the clients who were invited to the dinner. How can I win over the favor of the Roman people if my clients refuse to escort me to the forum? The room in which we were dining has been totally wrecked. How can I find new clients, if I am prevented from inviting them to dinner?

"Why didn't you hire acrobats? Acrobats don't criticize the guests. Acrobats don't incite the guests to fight. Acrobats please all Romans!

"But I know a very suitable punishment! You like (female) Greek philosophers? You praise the city of Athens? Excellent! You must set out for the city of Athens at once, and I don't want you ever to come back from there. Go!"

Answers to Comprehension Questions

1. Haterius feels he will have difficulty attaining the honors he wants now that the consul Sabinus, whose favor he wanted to win at the banquet, despises him. He feels he will have difficulty winning the favor of the Roman people because the clients he counted on to impress them by escorting him to the forum now mock him. And he will have difficulty attracting new clients since he cannot invite them to dinner with a dining-room in shambles.
2. Acrobats don't insult guests. Acrobats don't stir guests up to start fighting. All Romans like acrobats.
3. He orders Eryllus to go to Greece and never come back.
4. Eryllus is so fond of everything Greek (female philosophers and the city of Athens).

32.4 Haterius' Punishment

I

It was the middle of the night. After all the guests had returned home, Haterius was sitting alone in the dining-room, wondering what he was going to do. For while the guests were fighting, the dining-room had almost been destroyed. As the consul Sabinus was leaving the house, he had ordered Haterius not to invite him to dinner again. Euphrosyne, however, after seeing this, had departed with a calm expression in order to return to the harbor.

Haterius thought to himself, "I must punish that woman philosopher, who caused all this."

II

As day was dawning, Haterius set out very quickly for the River Tiber to find Euphrosyne. As the contractor was hurrying through the streets, he was cursing the woman philosopher and all Greeks:

"Greeks are very useless people: for they never work; they always think. Then, because they cannot agree about their opinions, they always fight among themselves. Now they are coming to our city, bringing these silly opinions...and now Romans are also fighting among themselves. I am going to arrest that philosopher and drag her to a judge, because she destroyed my dining-room."

When he came to the harbor, he boarded a ship at once to look for Euphrosyne very carefully. Suddenly Haterius caught sight of the girl going down into the hold and called in a loud voice,

"Wicked one! Why are you leaving the city? You must return with me! You ought to be punished, because you destroyed my home."

When the girl heard his shouting, she turned to Haterius and calmly prepared to return with him. Suddenly, however, both felt the ship moving.

"Hey!" shouted Haterius. "I have to get down from the ship!"

The terrified contractor began to run through the ship as quickly as he could. Then, after he reached the stern (of the ship), he jumped down into the river with a loud shout. There, he was thrashing about vigorously, cursing Euphrosyne and all philosophers.

Answers to Comprehension Questions

1. He set out for the harbor to look for Euphrosyne.
2. He was still angry at Euphrosyne and all Greeks.
3. He said they never worked, but just sat around thinking. Because they could not agree on their ideas, they ended up fighting with each other. Now they were bringing their silly ideas to Rome, and causing Romans to fight with each other. (*any two*)
4. He was going to arrest her and drag her to a judge for destroying his home.
5. He caught up to her heading down into the hold of a ship.
6. She calmly prepared to return with him.
7. The ship began to move.
8. He had jumped into the river and was thrashing about, cursing her and all philosophers.

34.1 A New Building

I

Salvius, after returning to his country villa, wanted to speak with his wife, Rufilla. He found her in the garden, waiting for Haterius and Vitellia.

"I bring excellent news!" he shouted. "With Paris killed and Domitia exiled, the emperor has promised me a consulship. However, I am worried about Haterius and your sister, who are still staying with us. If they return to the City, they will see a home which the actor set on fire and which the soldiers ransacked. It will be repaired in two months. How will we prevent them from learning the truth?"

II

After Salvius and Rufilla had discussed these matters for a short time, Haterius and Vitellia returned; they had been walking through the woods near the sea. As they entered the garden, Salvius met them, in order to greet them very happily.

"We are very fortunate," he exclaimed. "Because, at my suggestion, Domitia was able to be captured with Paris, the emperor has promised me a consulship. You also, my dear Haterius, will be honored with a reward."

Haterius, overcome with joy, could scarcely speak. Finally he asked his patron what kind of reward Domitian had chosen.

Salvius replied, "Because the emperor wants to forget his faithless wife, he has decided to build a new palace. He wants to inspect the island of Capri, where the Emperor Tiberius lived for many years. Would you be willing to sail to this island, stay there for two months, choose a suitable site, and make drawings? You will be allowed to take Vitellia with you."

Haterius and Vitellia could scarcely believe these words. Indeed, Vitellia asked Salvius,

"Surely you are joking?"

Salvius, however, replied calmly,

"I am speaking the truth. Because of my plans, the emperor himself said, 'A new building will be a suitable reward for Haterius.'"

Answers to Comprehension Questions

1 a He wanted to build a new palace.
   b He wanted to forget his faithless wife.
   c The emperor chose Capri because a previous emperor, Tiberius, had lived there for many years.
   d He hoped Haterius would be willing to sail to the island, stay there for two months, choose a suitable site, and draw up plans.

2 She found this so hard to believe that she asked Salvius if he was joking.

3 "A new building will be a suitable reward for Haterius," in actual fact would refer to the necessity of rebuilding Haterius' house following the damage done in carrying out the ambush on Domitia and Paris. (*We can assume that Salvius would have discussed this "collateral damage" with the emperor while reporting the success, otherwise, of his plot; and that the emperor would have seen the necessity and the wisdom of covering up the incident as thoroughly and as quickly as possible.*)

34.2 The Dwarf's Plan

I

As night was approaching, a young man was advancing quickly through the streets of the City. For, after receiving a strange letter, he had set out towards the River Tiber to meet the writer. As he was crossing a bridge, he caught sight of a light in the darkness.

"Quintus Caecilius Iucundus?" asked a voice.

Quintus made no reply. However, he wondered,

"What am I going to do if this man tries to kill me?"

Suddenly a dwarf appeared out of the darkness and ordered Quintus to follow him. Quintus, suspecting a trap, refused. The dwarf, therefore, so as not to frighten the young man, began to say these words calmly:

"I am Myropnous, a friend of Paris, the actor who was killed at the instigation of Gaius Salvius. Surely when that same Salvius arrived in Britain, he ordered King Cogidubnus, your friend, to be killed? If you help me, we will be able to prepare a suitable revenge. If you believe me, Salvius will soon be punished...and I will play the pipes again."

II

After Quintus heard these words, he began to laugh. For when Paris had died and Domitia had been exiled, rumors had spread through the whole City. Some people had suspected Epaphroditus, others the emperor himself. No one, however, had mentioned the name of Salvius. But Quintus, who had come to know this senator well, was easily able to believe Myropnous' words.

"My friend," he said, "I can trust you, and you me! I hate Salvius very much, because in Britain, after trying to kill not only a very loyal king but also me myself, he attempted to deceive Agricola, the Roman commander, about these matters. But we must be careful, because Salvius has a lot of influence with the emperor."

"Many men of the highest influence have been killed by emperors," replied Myropnous. "Vespasian, Domitian's father, ordered Helvidius Priscus, a very well-known senator, to be killed, after informers told about Helvidius' Stoic beliefs. Domitian, more than his father, is willing to welcome informers. Salvius, a very clever man, was eager to kill an actor and a king with his bold plans. Surely the emperor himself can also be killed by this clever man? If we tell Domitian this through informers whom the emperor trusts, he will soon suspect Salvius, will fear him...and will remove him! We must quickly 'warn' the emperor."

When Quintus had heard this (these words), he laughed.

"My friend," he said, "in a short time you will be playing the pipes again!"

Answers to Comprehension Questions

1 Some people said that Epaphroditus was responsible and others suspected the emperor himself.
2 In all the gossip, Salvius' name had never been mentioned.
3 Quintus knew Salvius well and therefore could easily believe that Myropnous' accusation was true.
4 He told Myropnous that Salvius had tried to kill him (Quintus) as well as the king. Then he had lied to Agricola about his actions.
5 Salvius had a lot of influence with the emperor.
6 Vespasian, Domitian's father, had ordered a senator, Helvidius Priscus, to be killed because informers had reported on Helvidius' Stoic beliefs. (*The Helvidii will appear in Unit 4.*)
7 He proposed using informers to suggest to Domitian that this clever man, whose plans included killing an actor and a king, might also be wanting to have the emperor killed.
8 When Myropnous had learned of Salvius' involvement in Paris' death, he vowed never to play the pipes again until Salvius was put to death.

34.3 Freedom

I

Cerialis, a slave who worked in the emperor's palace, wanted to be freed. Having written Domitian's letters for many years, he was wondering whether the emperor was ever going to give him his freedom. However, because he did not dare to ask a man of such great authority in person, he decided to write another letter, to send it to the emperor, and in this way to gain his freedom.

"Surely," the slave thought to himself, "if Domitian reads my words, he will reply quickly? If he gives me freedom, I will have to thank him. If he refuses, I will remain a slave."

Having said these words to himself, Cerialis prayed to the gods that Domitian would not refuse.

II

Titus Flavius Cerialis, imperial freedman (freedman of Augustus), was walking happily through Domitian's palace. In his hands he carried many letters dictated by the emperor. In his bedroom, however, he kept one letter, in which the emperor had promised him his freedom. For when Domitian had received Cerialis' letter, delighted by the bold plan, he had summoned the slave himself and had dictated a letter to Cerialis, offering him freedom. Cerialis guarded this letter with his life!

But after Cerialis was freed by Domitian, he had caught sight of a very beautiful slave-girl in the palace one day and had fallen in love with her. This slave-girl, named Philaenis, was Domitia's hairdresser. When he saw her, Cerialis had again thought to himself,

"Alas! What a beautiful girl! Freedmen, however, are not allowed to marry slave-girls. Slaves can possess slave-girls as 'partners.' But I am not a slave! Why did I seek my freedom?

"…But I have a plan. I will save up money and write another letter to the emperor. If he allows me, I am going to buy freedom for Philaenis."

Therefore the imperial freedman was walking happily through Domitian's palace.

Answers to Comprehension Questions

1 He now has three names (Titus Flavius Cerialis) and is also described as an imperial freedman.
2 He was delighted by Cerialis' bold plan of asking for his freedom in a letter.
3 He summoned Cerialis and dictated a letter to him in which he offered the slave freedom.
4 He kept this letter in his bedroom and "guarded it with his life."
5 He had fallen in love with a beautiful slave-girl, who was Domitia's hairdresser.
6 Freedmen cannot marry slaves (or slave-girls). If he were still a slave, he could at least have Philaenis as a "common-law" partner.
7 He was going to save up some money and write a letter to the emperor, asking to buy Philaenis' freedom.

The story in 34.3 was inspired by the last tombstone on page 288 of the Student Text (reproduced here on page 50).

34.4 Many Strange Events

I

At the first hour of the day, Quintus Haterius Latronianus, worn out with worries, was wandering near the Tiber River. For because his dining-room had been ransacked by the guests and the doorway almost destroyed by flames (while Domitia and Paris were trying to escape), he was wondering why the gods were punishing him. As the contractor was contemplating this, he suddenly caught sight of a body lying underneath a bridge.

"Good God!" Haterius said to himself. "It is Euphrosyne, the female philosopher whom I was going to punish. If anyone finds me near the body, I will be thrown into prison. How was this body placed here? Who did it? What else will happen to me?"

Then he said to himself, "Perhaps I should throw the body into the river."

II

As Haterius was about to drag the body to the river bank, he caught sight of three friends approaching the bridge. He quickly hid under the bridge, wondering whether the friends could see the body. However, because they were talking intently to each other, they crossed the bridge unaware.

Haterius said to himself, "It is dangerous for the body to be dragged to the river. Perhaps I should run away as quickly as possible...but if anyone sees me running from the bridge, he will arrest me. Perhaps it is better to walk along through the streets slowly as if I had seen nothing remarkable."

As Haterius was thinking this over, Gaius Salvius Liberalis approached the bridge. When Haterius had seen him, he said,

"It is all over with me! Unless I avoid my patron, he will doubtlessly suspect me. Where shall I flee?"

But Salvius had seen Haterius...and the philosopher's body; he ordered his client not to run away. He congratulated the wretched contractor in this way:

"I recognize this girl, not only

beautiful but dangerous. She is a Stoic philosopher, an enemy to the Emperor Domitian. He will thank you very much, when he hears about her death. We must hurry to the palace!"

And the patron led his stunned client to the emperor.

Answers to Comprehension Questions

1 Three friends approached the bridge.
2 He thought perhaps he should just run away.
3 If anyone saw him running from the bridge, he would likely be arrested (especially if the body was also found).
4 He could perhaps try to walk slowly through the streets as if he had seen nothing amazing.
5 Salvius approached...and caught sight of him (and the body).
6 It turned out that, according to Salvius, Euphrosyne, as a Stoic philosopher, was inimical to the emperor. Domitian would thank Haterius for getting rid of her. Far from being arrested, Haterius was likely to be rewarded, even though he was not actually guilty of killing the woman.

34.5 Threatening Inscriptions

I

After Salvius was made consul by the Emperor Domitian, he usually went to the forum every day. One day, as he was entering the senate-house, he caught sight of a new inscription written on the wall:

There will be no escape!

When the other senators had seen this inscription, they asked each other who had written these words and what they meant. Salvius, however, in a loud voice called for silence.

"Friends," he shouted, "we must look at this inscription carefully. We have already seen the same inscription on other buildings throughout the city. Whoever wrote this is going to write more inscriptions. If we find the meaning of these words, we will come up with a plan by which this rogue can be arrested. Then he will be quickly removed!"

While Salvius was saying this, the senators had begun to laugh. But he urged them not to laugh until (before) they had punished the author of the inscriptions.

II

After Salvius had returned home, he talked to his wife, Rufilla, about the inscriptions. He said nothing about the opinions of the senators because it is not proper for a senator to speak with his wife about senatorial matters. When Rufilla heard the words of the inscriptions: 'There will be no escape!', she exclaimed,

"My sister, Vitellia, mentioned these words when she was telling about the actor, Paris. A certain freedman, obviously a Christian, threatened her friends because they were praising Paris. He warned the actor not to continue with his sins, if he did not want to be punished by God. He threatened 'flames sent from heaven' and 'no escape.'"

"Excellent!" shouted Salvius. "Who was this freedman? Did Vitellia mention his name?"

"Clito...Tychlito...I have forgotten," replied his wife. "But he was a client of Titus Flavius Clemens. I remember this."

"Then I must hurry to Clemens," chortled Salvius. "My dearest freedman, you believe in one God? You thank this God because Paris has died? You now dare to threaten us senators? You must

beware. I, not your God, was the author of Paris' demise. And I will also be the author of your death."

Answers to Comprehension Questions

1   It was not proper for senators to discuss senatorial business with their wives.
2   Her sister Vitellia had mentioned the phrase when she was talking about the actor, Paris.
3   When Vitellia's friends were praising Paris (1), a freedman had used this phrase and also 'flames sent from heaven (1)' to threaten the actor (1) unless he discontinued his sinning ways (1). (any three points)
4   The freedman was a client of Titus Flavius Clemens.
5   Because Tychicus believed in one God, he also probably believed this God, in response to Tychicus' warnings, had sent the punishment by which Paris died. Now he was threatening the people of Rome with the signs because he was confident that his God would also support his threats against them.
6   His news was that he, not Tychicus' God, was responsible for Paris' death. His warning was that he would also be responsible for Tychicus' death.

36.1 A Stupid Poet

I

The poet Martial is hurrying through the city in order to visit a friend. He is carrying a new booklet with him because he knows well that this friend admires epigrams. As he is crossing through the forum, he notices that a large crowd near the Rostra is laughing and shouting.

"I think that I should approach nearer," he says to himself, "in order to find out why this crowd is aroused/excited. For I suspect that something silly is happening...and you, Martial, know that you are always attracted by silly things."

II

After the poet gets closer, he catches sight of an old man standing on the Rostra in order to recite from a booklet. However, whenever he makes a start to his recitation, the crowd laughs loudly. Finally, when everyone is quiet for a short time, the old man begins:

"You say that the pretty girls burn
    with love for you, Sextus,
Who have the face of someone
    swimming without water."

At first the listeners say nothing, because they cannot understand these words.

One of the listeners says, "How can Sextus swim without water? This epigram is stupid."

Then the listeners begin to curse and mock the old man.

Martial, who is now getting angry, says to himself:

"This old man is so stupid that he steals my epigrams but doesn't understand the words. Sextus is swimming *under* water, not *without* water. Blockhead!"

While Martial is thinking this to himself, the old man tries to recite another epigram:

"Quintus loves Thais. 'Which Thais?'
    'Blind Thais.'
That Thais has no eye, he has two."

Martial, who can no longer / cannot now contain himself, exclaims:

"Enough! Enough! This donkey is destroying my epigrams! Friends! I urge you to listen to me."

The listeners, who recognize Martial, are quiet, so that the poet may speak.

Looking intently at the old man, he shouts:

"Who are you, little man?"

"I am Fidentinus," says the old man, blushing.

"You recite badly, friend," replies Martial, "but perhaps you are recited better. Listen to this!

The booklet which you recite is mine,
    O Fidentinus;
But when you recite badly, it
    begins to be yours."

After Martial says these words, the listeners laugh, applaud, and chase the old man out of the forum.

Answers to Comprehension Questions

1 He is able to see an old man standing on the Rostra in order to recite from a booklet.
2 Every time the man starts to recite, the crowd laughs loudly.
3 Martial wrote that Sextus had the face of someone swimming under water. This man has him swimming without water.
4 The one listener thinks the poem is stupid.
5 Martial calls the poet stupid for stealing his poems without understanding what they mean.
6 In Martial's original, Thais is lacking one eye, and Quintus must be lacking two for falling in love with her. The old man completely misses the point by simply saying that Thais is blind and Quintus has two eyes.
7 He interrupts proceedings and asks everyone to listen to him.
8 The crowd is silent, because they recognize Martial.
9 The little book which you recite is mine, Fidentinus,
But when you recite badly, it begins to be yours.

10 The crowd laughs and applauds...and then chases the old man out of the forum.

A dialogue version of this story appears in the Unit 4 Omnibus Workbook *(36.1: poēta vērus). Do not use the version above for evaluation purposes if you have already used the* **OW** *version. However, the* **OW** *version could be used for oral practice after completing this version.*

36.2 About the Poet, Martial

I

Martial is sitting in his study in order to write this letter to his friend, Juvenal:

"When you were being bothered by the noises and the crowds of the City, I was returning to my homeland, Spain. Do you know that I can now sleep until the third hour (until 9:00 a.m.)? Can you believe that the neighbours do not urge me to wear my toga all the time? The cook, who understands that I am fond of hunting in the woods, prepares such good food that I am often forgetful of the animals. I will be happy to live and to die in this way."

II

After Martial returned to Spain, he died in a few years. After his death, Gaius Plinius Secundus, a very famous writer and a friend of Martial, composed a letter in order to praise the dead poet's talent and skill. He did this because Martial, a few years earlier, had composed an epigram praising Pliny (Plinius).

Do you believe that all Roman citizens agree with Pliny? Read these words in order to decide whether Fabulla, an old woman, would agree:

You have either all old friends
Or (ones that are) disgusting and more
    repulsive than old people;
You bring these as your companions
    and you drag them with you
Through parties, colonnades and
    theaters:
In this way, Fabulla, you are beautiful,
    you are a girl.

Laetinus, an old man, also thinks his friends can be deceived. Would he like to read these lines?

Laetinus, you lie (about) your youth
    with dyed hair,
So suddenly a crow who were recently
    a swan.
You don't fool everyone; Proserpina
    knows you are gray-haired:
She will pull down the mask from
    your head.

Martial also writes that Linus, a rich man, makes fun of his villa (which he calls a "farm"). Because Linus often asks why the poet stays in such a small villa, he is punished in this way:

Linus, you ask what my farm at
    Nomentum returns to me?
My farm returns me this: I don't see
    you, Linus!

However, all these people are now very famous citizens because of Martial's epigrams. Perhaps they can say about him just as he can about them:

You are difficult and easy, sweet and
    sour at the same time;
I can live neither with you nor
    without you.

Answers to Comprehension Questions

1 He wrote a letter praising Martial's talent and skill, because, a few years earlier, Martial had written an epigram praising Pliny.

2 She wants people to think that she is young and beautiful.

3 She surrounds herself with people who are older and uglier than she is.

4 He dyes his hair.

5 Martial says he is now suddenly a crow (black-haired), but was recently a swan (white-haired).

6 Since Proserpina rules in the Underworld, Martial probably means Laetinus will die soon. (That will prove he is really older than he pretends to be.)

7 He calls it a "farm." He asks why Martial stays in such a small villa. (either point)

8 When Martial is at his villa, he doesn't have to see Linus!

9 Martial has made them all famous/infamous/immortal through his poetry.

10 Without Martial, whom they dislike for insulting them in his poetry, they would not be remembered by posterity. Without their foibles, Martial would not have anyone to write about (and himself would not have become famous through the years).

The first two poems in Part II are Martial VIII.79 and III.43. The third and fourth poems in Part II are included in the Unit 4 Omnibus Workbook (36.2 More of Martial's Art). Part I and Part II can each be done as separate items, if teachers wish.

37.1 A Very Useful Freedman

I

Epaphroditus is hurrying through the atrium of the palace. For he has been summoned by the emperor in the middle of the night and he does not know why Domitian wants to speak with him. He believes, however, that the emperor has decided to recall his wife. He enters the bedroom in order to talk with Domitian:

Domitian: My dear Epaphroditus, I cannot sleep, because Domitia isn't here. I think that she ought to be recalled.

Epaphroditus: But, sir, if you recall her so quickly, all the Romans will laugh at you. For you know that when Paris was killed and Domitia exiled, you were saved from great danger. But now another actor, very much like Paris, has caused you to think about Domitia. I will give orders that he be killed.

II

When this actor has been killed, the emperor is silent about Domitia for a short time. One day, Aelius Lamia, Domitia's first husband, meets him. For Domitia divorced Aelius so that she could be married by Domitian. Catching sight of Aelius, the emperor asks:

Domitian: After Domitia divorced you, did you marry anyone else?

Aelius: Why do you ask, sir? Perhaps you are looking for another wife?

Domitian, stricken with anger, gives orders to Epaphroditus that Aelius be removed. When this is done, the emperor remains content for a few days. Then he summons his freedman again:

Domitian: (*holding a booklet*) Who wrote this booklet?

Epaphroditus: Why do you ask, sir?

Domitian: Here! Read here! The author tells that Paris, the Trojan prince, divorced his wife, Oenone. Don't you think that the author is really talking about Domitia and me? Besides, Paris was the name of the actor whom Domitia loved. I certainly believe that this author is making fun of me.

Epaphroditus: Helvidius Priscus wrote

this booklet. His family is dangerous.
I will give orders that he be killed.

Domitian: (*when Epaphroditus has left*)
You are a very useful freedman,
Epaphroditus. You even helped the
Emperor Nero, when you offered him
a dagger with which to kill himself.
But one day I will give orders that you
be killed, Epaphroditus, because I
don't want you to offer me a dagger
also.

Answers to Comprehension Questions

1   Aelius Lamia is Domitia's first
husband (whom she divorced to
marry Domitian).
2   He asks Aelius Lamia if he has
married anyone else since Domitia
divorced him.
3   He asks Domitian if he is looking for
another wife.
4   He orders Epaphroditus to have
Aelius killed.
5   The book is about the Trojan hero,
Paris, divorcing his wife, Oenone.
6   He thinks the book is making fun of
him. Because Paris was also the name
of the actor Domitia loved, Domitian
thinks the book is really about
Domitia and himself.
7   He says the writer is Helvidius
Priscus, from a dangerous family.
8   He will issue orders that Helvidius is
to be killed.
9   He helped the Emperor Nero commit
suicide by offering him a dagger with
which to do the deed.
10   Some day he will issue orders that
Epaphroditus is to be killed.
11   He doesn't want a situation to develop
where Epaphroditus will also be
offering him a dagger (to help him
commit suicide).

37.2 About Agricola's Good Fortune

I

Agricola was born (had been born) when
Gaius Caesar was consul for the third
time, on June 13; he died in his fifty-
fourth year, on August 23, when Collega
and Priscinus were consuls. Perhaps
posterity would like to know that his
personal appearance was quite
handsome, rather than quite imposing;
nothing violent was seen in his face;
kindliness of expression remained. It was
easy to believe that he was a good man; it
was pleasant to believe that he was a
great man. Although he himself was
snatched from us at the mid-point of his
prime (of life), nevertheless, because of
his well-deserved fame, he lived a "very
long" life. Endowed with consular and
triumphal distinctions, having obtained
enough money, with his daughter and
wife still living, he died fortunate, before
the evil deeds of a very cruel emperor
could harm him.

Answers to Comprehension Questions

1   He dates them by the men who were
consuls in those years.
2   He was in his fifty-fourth year (he was
53).
3   He was handsome, rather than
imposing, with kindliness rather than
violence in his expression.
4   Tacitus thinks posterity might be
interested in these details.
5   He was a good man.
6   He was a great man.
7   Because of his well-deserved fame, his
life was very long (possibly meaning
that he will live on in memory long
after his physical death, or perhaps
simply that he accomplished much
more in his 53 years than most people
do in much longer lives).

8 He had enjoyed the rank of consul and the honor of a triumph (political/military success); he had been able to make enough money for his needs (financial success); his wife and daughter were still alive; and he died before the evil deeds of a very cruel emperor could harm him.

II

We, not Agricola, see that the senate-house has been besieged and the senate surrounded by soldiers; we learn about the death of so many men of consular rank and about the exile of so many very noble women. We know that the opinions/pronouncements of Catullus Messalinus did not yet reach the senate-house while Agricola was being honored by the emperor; that Helvidius was not yet thrown into prison; that Flavius Clemens and Acilius Glabrio were not yet killed.

When Nero was emperor, he turned away his eyes and ordered but did not watch his crimes. Domitian, however, not only watches, but is present in order to note whether any friends, by their pale expression, indicate that they support the victim and despise the emperor.

37.2 can be done as a companion activity to Omnibus Workbook *37.4 on Agricola's death.*

38.1 A Dangerous Letter

I

Gaius Helvidius Lupus sends greetings to his friend, Acilius Glabrio.

I know for certain that when you have read my words, you will weep. For I announce to you that my son has died. Perhaps you remember that he left our villa and visited some girl in the city.

I don't know why he fell in love with a girl who is a relative of the emperor. I don't know why he forgot that the emperor hates our family. But I do know that the mind is often ruled by the heart.

II

Polla, the girl whom my son loved, is the daughter of Titus Flavius Clemens. Domitian, an idiot who thinks that relatives (like the rest of the Romans) are slaves, gave orders to Clemens that Polla should marry Sparsus. Consider the stupidity of the man! He knows well that Polla is fourteen years old and Sparsus fifty. Nevertheless, because he says that he is going to adopt Clemens' sons, he believes that he also owns the daughter.

My son could not understand why Polla had been prevented from marrying him. Therefore, on the day when she was about to marry Sparsus, he set out for Sparsus' home and attacked him with a dagger, as he was standing in front of the doorway. Then, after he was overpowered by slaves, he was led to the emperor, who ordered him to be killed.

The father of this emperor once sent my father to his death; now his son has killed my son. I myself want to kill that beast. Are you astonished? I, who have often warned you not to offend the emperor, who have often written to you to be careful, now openly curse and accuse Domitian? I don't care! Just as my son loved Polla, I loved my son. Just as my father and my son were not afraid of death, I also dare to die. Do not warn me to beware! Let the emperor beware! Good-bye!

Answers to Comprehension Questions

1 Helvidius feels the emperor treats relatives (and all Romans) like slaves.

2 The emperor ordered Polla to marry a much older man (14 years old vs. 50).

3 The emperor feels that because he has promised to adopt Clemens' two sons, he can also make decisions about Clemens' daughter (as if he owned her also).

4 Helvidius suggests that his son could not understand why Polla couldn't marry him.

5 The son's attack on Sparsus with a dagger, his overpowering by family slaves and his having been sent off to the emperor are all mentioned in our story. (*any one detail*)

6 The story in our text does not mention that the emperor ordered the son to be killed.

7 Helvidius wishes to kill the emperor (that beast).

8 He has often warned Glabrio against offending the emperor and has repeatedly told him to be careful.

9 Just as his son loved Polla, he loved his son. Just as his father and son were not afraid to die, he too dares to perish.

10 He tells Glabrio not to warn him to beware.

11 Let the emperor beware!

The selections from Stage 38 are based to some extent on real incidents, even if the Polla–Helvidius love story from our texts is fiction. See the notes in the Teacher's Manual *for some background on Glabrio, Helvidius, and Clemens.*

38.2 An Argument

I

Polla, the daughter of Titus Flavius Clemens, is complaining to her father about her husband, Sparsus. Because Clemens knows that Polla married Sparsus unwillingly, he does not want to talk about this matter. However, she begs her father to listen to her words:

Polla: I do not know, father, why I was forced to marry that old man. I do not know why you have made life very wretched for me. I only know that this traitor never stays in our house through the night; that he has often been seen with other women; that for these reasons I am mocked by my friends. Indeed, I believe that I will kill that man...or myself...if he does not put an end to this treachery.

Clemens: Although you are very upset, my dear Polla, it is useless to complain. I myself am forced to take many hateful actions (to do many hateful things) so that the Emperor Domitian won't punish my family. Surely you agree that even a very wretched life is better than no life?

II

Polla: Father, you are very cowardly! I prefer death to a very wretched life. Surely you have not forgotten that Helvidius, whom I loved very much, perished, killed by praetorian soldiers? You ought to understand that I too am not afraid of death.

Clemens: Why do you mention that young man? Helvidius was obviously very stupid, not very brave, just like his grandfather, who, although he was a very well-known senator, dared to curse the Emperor Vespasian and paid the penalty with his death; and just like his uncle, who, because he puts on / has put on plays in the theater, which seem to make fun of the emperor's family, offends Domitian very much. I cannot understand why you praise this family.

Polla: I praise Helvidius' family, because those men know how to die bravely. Without a doubt, you will die ignominiously, just like your brother. When he was elected consul, he incurred Domitian's hatred, because

108

the herald accidentally used the word "imperator/emperor" instead of "consul." To agree always with such an emperor is not only cowardly but also useless.

Clemens: And to disagree with such an emperor is also useless. Domitian himself chose your husband. If you kill Sparsus, or yourself, you will also kill your father and your mother, because of the emperor's anger. You must choose...

Answers to Comprehension Questions

1 She says that she prefers death to a very wretched life. (She calls her father a coward for thinking the opposite.)

2 Since Helvidius, the man she loved, was killed by praetorian soldiers, her father should not be surprised that she also does not fear death.

3 He calls Helvidius and his family very stupid, not very brave.

4 The young man's grandfather was put to death by Vespasian. Although he was a very well-known senator, he dared to curse the emperor and was punished accordingly. The young man's uncle puts on plays in the theater which appear to make fun of the imperial family, hence offending Domitian. (either of these examples)

5 She calls them cowardly. She says that Helvidius' family know how to die bravely.

6 When her uncle was named consul, he incurred Domitian's anger because the person making the announcement accidentally used the word "emperor" instead of the word "consul." The uncle died as a result. Trying to humor an emperor who would behave this way is not only cowardly but useless.

7 He tells his daughter that if she kills Sparsus or herself, she will also be killing her parents, because of the emperor's anger at such resistance to his choice of husband.

39.1 A Teacher Tricked

I

Titus and Publius, the sons of Clemens, are reading a booklet of the poet, Ovid, in order to recite the lines for their teacher, Quintilian, the next day. Because Titus knows that the teacher will ask him to recite first, he complains to his brother:

Titus: My dear Publius, don't you think this Quintilian is a very stupid man? For although you are afraid that you may have to recite first, you are always asked after me.

Publius: I believe the teacher has always done this because you, being older, recite better. I also notice that when the speeches are finished, you are praised more often than I am.

Titus: I have an idea, therefore! Tomorrow we will be asked to recite these verses. Quintilian won't ask if we have learned the whole thing. If I prepare the first part of the poem and you the second, the teacher will never realize that he has been tricked.

Publius: Okay!

II

The next day, the boys return to the palace and are greeted by Quintilian.

Quintilian: Hello, Titus and Publius! Yesterday, you were trying to learn some lines of the poet, Ovid. I hope that you can recite this poem today. But first I would like to hear this story in your own words and in prose speech. Titus, begin!

Titus: Pyramus, the most handsome of young men, and Thisbe, surpassing all (other) girls, lived in (owned) adjoining houses. In time their love grew...but their fathers forbade marriage! However, although the lovers were not permitted to visit each other, by placing their lips on a thin crack of the common wall, they often whispered and gave kisses. At length, led on by love and boldness, they decided that one quiet night they would try to trick the guards and go out, and would meet outside the city under the shade of a very well-known tree:

There a tree, very rich in snow-white fruit, was a tall mulberry, close to a cold spring.

That night Thisbe, whom love was making bold, arrived at the tree first. Look! A lioness, smeared with the recent killing of oxen, came to drink the water of the spring.

Babylonian Thisbe saw it from a distance in the rays of the moon (in the moonlight), fled on trembling feet into a dark cave, and while she fled, left behind her veil which had slipped from her back.

Pyramus, who had left home later, came to the tree. When he found the clothing stained with blood (because the lioness had torn the veil with her bloody mouth), he feared that Thisbe had died.

He said, "One night will destroy two lovers!"

Having said this, and having given kisses to the clothing, he killed himself with a sword.

The fruit of the tree turned to a dark appearance with the spray of the killing and the root, wet with blood, dyed the hanging fruit with a deep red color.

Titus stops speaking because he believes the teacher will ask Publius to narrate the rest of the lines. Quintilian, however, signals Titus to resume his speech. Because he has entrusted the rest of the lines to his brother, he doesn't know what to say (what he is to say). However, he comes up with an idea quickly and explains to Quintilian:

Titus: Sir, I cannot resume this story. Whenever I am telling about Pyramus and Thisbe, I think about Polla, our sister, and her beloved Helvidius. A difficult thing...

Quintilian, who understands about Polla's love and Helvidius' death, is tricked by these words. Afterwards, however, Titus and Publius learn all the lines!

Answers to Comprehension Questions

1   He wants the boys to tell the story in their own words and in prose speech.
2   Pyramus was the most handsome of young men, and Thisbe surpassed all other girls.
3   They lived in adjoining houses.
4   Their fathers refused to let them marry (or even visit each other).
5   By pressing their lips to a crack in the common wall, they whispered to each other and gave each other kisses.
6   They would try to trick the guards, get out, and meet at an agreed-upon spot.
7   There was a tall mulberry tree there (thick with fruit) and also a cold spring near-by.
8   She got there first, but saw a lioness fresh from a kill, coming to drink from the spring.
9   She fled into a cave.
10   He was afraid that Thisbe had died (been killed).
11   He saw her veil stained with blood but did not realize she had dropped it as she fled and the lioness had torn it with its blood-stained mouth.

12 He killed himself with a sword.

13 The fruit of the mulberry tree used to be snow-white, but it turned to deep red (to a dark color) when it was spattered by Pyramus' blood.

14 He says that he cannot continue because the story reminds him too much of his sister Polla's love for Helvidius and of Helvidius' death.

15 After this, they learn all the lines of poetry that are assigned.

If students want to know the full version of Ovid's tale, refer them to Metamorphoses *IV.55ff. The lines quoted by Titus are 89–90, 99–101, 108, and 125–7.*

40.1 A Very Wretched Patron

I

When Gaius Salvius Liberalis understood that he was being sent into exile, he summoned his son and a few friends who had helped him, in order to thank them. With his son standing by, he declared that he had always supported them and that he would never forget their support.

He said, "If you are afraid that the emperor may also punish you, I urge you to follow me into exile."

Haterius, Salvius' client, by stepping forward quickly, joined his patron.

II

The next day, Haterius entered Salvius' house and found his patron intently looking at a book. Salvius, catching sight of his client, sadly announced that he was reading the words of the poet, Ovid.

He said, "Ovid was also condemned to exile by his emperor, and he wrote these verses in order to say good-bye to his family and his friends:

As I am about to leave, I speak for the last time to my sad friends, who, reduced from many recently, were one or two. My loving wife, weeping more bitterly herself, held me, weeping, as tears fell continually down guiltless cheeks. My daughter was far away in African lands and could not be informed of my fate."

After Salvius had recited these words, he put the book down on a couch and burst into tears.

Answers to Comprehension Questions

1 He was looking intently at a book (of Ovid's poetry).

2 The lines were written to say good-bye to Ovid's family and friends.

3 Like Ovid, Salvius has seen the number of his friends dwindle, perhaps down to just Haterius.

4 Ovid's wife held her husband and shared in his weeping. Rufilla had deserted Salvius when things got tough.

5 Ovid's daughter was away in Africa and did not know of her father's fate. Salvius' son is standing by to support him as he prepares to leave.

6 He set the book down and burst into tears.

The poem is from Ovid, Tristia *I.3.15–20.*

40.2 Haterius Reconsiders

I

After Quintus Haterius Latronianus promised Salvius that he would accompany his patron into exile, he hurried home to announce this to his wife. When Vitellia heard this plan, she thought that her husband had been affected by insanity. She could not believe that he was considering such a journey.

She said, "Do you understand that by following your patron you have betrayed your wife and your family? Besides, I am afraid that, if you leave, the emperor may punish all of us."

II

After Vitellia said these words, she hurried from the house and headed for her father's home, in order to look for her sister, Rufilla. Haterius was left alone in the house and began to read a book, in which he found verses of the poet Ovid:

But when sad winter has revealed its rough face, and the earth has become bright with frost like marble, hairs, with ice hanging down, often resound when they are moved; and the white beard shines when frost has been spread over it; and bare wines freeze, keeping the shape of their jug; and instead of draughts of wine, people drink morsels that they have been given. Why should I say how the streams harden, enchained by the cold, and crackling waters (ice) are dug from the lake?

While Haterius was inspecting these words, he became terrified. For the poet, Ovid, was telling about his own exile. Haterius began to fear that he would be leaving with Salvius for a similar country. Leaving the book in the house, he headed for Vitellia's father's home to search for his wife.

Answers to Comprehension Questions

1 She left the house and headed for her father's home.
2 She was going to look for her sister, Rufilla.
3 Left alone in the house, he started to read some lines by the poet, Ovid.
4 a The hairs resound because of the icicles hanging down from them (and hitting each other when the hairs move).
  b There is a layer of frost covering the beard and making it glisten.
  c The wine freezes in the shape of its jug (even when there is no jug holding it).
  d They "drink" solid pieces rather than liquid.
  e Ice is being cut from the lake (as is still done in some locations, to serve as blocks of ice in ice houses through the summer months).
5 He began to worry that he might have agreed to be exiled in a similar climate.
6 He headed for Vitellia's father's home to search for her.

The poem is from Ovid, Tristia III.10.9–10, 21–6.